tar Cho ok

Hillsong
United

Cover photo by Tommy McNamara

ISBN 978-1-4234-3239-5

HAL•LEONARD®
CORPORATION
7777 W. BLUEMOUND RD. P.O. BOX 13819 MILWAUKEE, WI 53213

Contents

All About You

Words and Music by
Joel Houston

Melody:

Hear _ our prais - es, __   hear _ Your

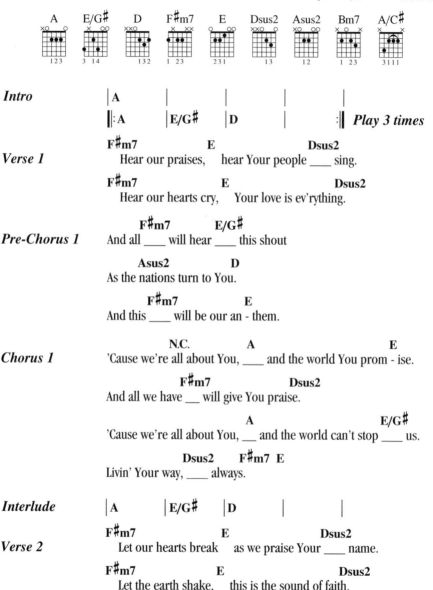

A   E/G#   D   F#m7   E   Dsus2   Asus2   Bm7   A/C#

Intro
|A | | | |
||: A | E/G# | D | :|| *Play 3 times*

Verse 1
          F#m7   E   Dsus2
          Hear our praises,   hear Your people ___ sing.

          F#m7   E   Dsus2
          Hear our hearts cry,   Your love is ev'rything.

Pre-Chorus 1
                    F#m7   E/G#
          And all ___ will hear ___ this shout

                    Asus2   D
          As the nations turn to You.

                    F#m7   E
          And this ___ will be our an - them.

Chorus 1
                    N.C.   A   E
          'Cause we're all about You, ___ and the world You prom - ise.

                    F#m7   Dsus2
          And all we have __ will give You praise.

                              A   E/G#
          'Cause we're all about You, __ and the world can't stop ___ us.

                    Dsus2   F#m7 E
          Livin' Your way, ___ always.

Interlude
|A | E/G# | D | |

Verse 2
          F#m7   E   Dsus2
          Let our hearts break   as we praise Your ___ name.

          F#m7   E   Dsus2
          Let the earth shake,   this is the sound of faith.

Pre-Chorus 2   *Repeat Pre-Chorus 1*

Chorus 2   *Repeat Chorus 1*

           Bm7   **F♯m7**   **D**

Bridge   And the walls will fall down, ___ and religion will ___ break.

           Bm7   **F♯m7**

     And the nations will hear ___ this shout.

          D

     Can you hear the sound of faith?

                         F♯m7

Pre-Chorus 3 ‖: 'Cause we're all about You.

        E   **D**

     'Cause we're all about ___ You. :‖ *Play 4 times*

                 N.C.   **A**   **E**

Chorus 3   'Cause we're all about You, ___ and the world You prom - ise.

                F♯m7   **Dsus2**

     And all we have __ will give You praise.

                          A   **E/G♯**

     'Cause we're all about You, __ and the world can't stop ___ us.

              Dsus2   **F♯m7**

     Livin' Your way, ___ always.

                E   **A**

     'Cause we're all about You.

     E/G♯   **Dsus2**

      'Cause we're all about ___ You.

                        A

     'Cause we're all about You.

     E/G♯   **Dsus2**

      'Cause we're all about ___ You.

           A   **E/G♯**

Outro   ‖: And all the walls are fall - ing down,

     A/C♯   **D**

     As all the nations praise.

      A   **E/G♯**

     And all the world will hear ___ this shout,

      Dsus2

     Can you hear the sound of faith? :‖

All Day

Words and Music by
Marty Sampson

Melody:

I don't care _ what they say a - bout me, _

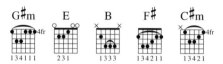

G#m   E   B   F#   C#m

Intro

‖: N.C.(G#m) (E) |(B)   (F#)   :‖ *Play 4 times*

Verse 1

G#m   E   B   F#
  I don't care what they say about me,

  G#m   E B   F#
It's al - right,   it's al - right.

G#m   E   B   F#
  I don't care what they think about me,

  G#m   E   B   F#
It's al - right,   they'll get it one day.

G#m   E   B   F#   G#m
  'Cause I love You,   And I'll follow You.

   E   B   F#
You are my,   my life.

G#m   E   B   F#
  And I will read my Bible and pray,

G#m E   B   F#
I will   follow You all day.

Interlude 1

‖: G#m   E |B   F#   :‖

Verse 2

G#m   E   B   F#
And I don't care what it costs anymore,

    G#m   E   B   F#
'Cause You gave it all, ___ and I'm following You.

G#m E   B   F#
I don't care what it takes anymore,

    G#m   E   B   F#
No matter what happens I'm going Your way.

G#m   E   B   F#   G#m
  'Cause I love You,   And I'll follow You.

    E   B   F#
You are my,   my life.

G#m   E   B   F#
  And I will read my Bible and pray,

G#m E   B   F#
I will   follow You all day.

Chorus 1

B   E B   F#   B   E G#m E
All day,   all day now, ___ all day. (I will follow you.)

B   E B   F#   B   E G#m E
All day,   all day now, ___ all day. (I will follow you.)

Interlude 2   *Repeat Interlude 1*

Verse 3   *Repeat Verse 1*

Chorus 2   *Repeat Chorus 1*

Bridge

C#m   E   C#m
  Anyone ___ around can see

        E   C#m
Just how good You've been to me.

        E   C#m
For all my friends who don't know You

        E   B
I pray that You would save them too.

Outro   *Repeat Chorus 1 till fade*

All For Love

Words and Music by
Mia Fieldes

Melody:

All for love __ a Fa-ther gave, __

(Capo 2nd fret)

Fmaj7   G6/B   C   Fmaj7/A   Am7   G   D/F#   Em   Em9

Intro

| Fmaj7 G6/B | C | Fmaj7/A G6/B | C |

Verse 1

Fmaj7   G6/B   C
All for love ____ a Father gave,

Fmaj7   G6/B   Am7
For only love ____ can make a way.

Fmaj7   G6/B   Am7
All for love ____ the heavens cried,

Fmaj7   G6/B   C
For love ____ was crucified.

Pre-Chorus 1

             G6/B   Am7
Oh, how many times ____ have I broken Your heart,

               Fmaj7   C
But still You forgive ____ if only I ask?

              G6/B   Am7
And how many times ____ have You heard me pray?

       Fmaj7
Draw near ____ to me.

Chorus 1

   G   D/F#   Em
Ev'rything I need ____ is You,

                 C
My beginning, my for - ever.

   G   D/F#   Em   C
Ev'rything I need ____ is You.

Verse 2

Fmaj7   G6/B   C
Let me sing, ___ all for love.

Fmaj7 G6/B   C
I will join the angel song.

Fmaj7 G6/B   Am7
Ever ho - ly is the Lord.

Fmaj7   G6/B   C
King of glo - ry, King of all.

Pre-Chorus 2   *Repeat Pre-Chorus 1*

Chorus 2   *Repeat Chorus 1 (Play 2 times)*

Interlude   ‖: Em | |C | :‖
     | | |

Verse 3

C   D/F#   G
All for love ___ a Saviour prayed,

C   D/F#   G
Abba Fa - ther, have Your way.

C   D/F#   G
Though they know ___ not what they do,

C   D/F#   Em9
Let the cross ___ draw man to You,

To You, to You, to You.

Chorus 3   *Repeat Chorus 1 (Play 2 times)*

All I Need Is You

Words and Music by
Marty Sampson

Melody:

Left my fear by the side of the road, _

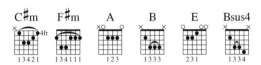

C#m   F#m   A   B   E   Bsus4

Intro |C#m F#m |A   B |C#m E |Bsus4 B |

Verse 1

    C#m   F#m
Left my fear by the side of the road,

    A   B
Hear You speak, won't let go.

    C#m   E   Bsus4 B
Fall to my knees, as I lift my hands to pray,

    C#m   F#m
Got ev'ry reason to be here again.

     A   B
A Father's love that draws me in,

     C#m   E   Bsus4
And all my eyes wanna see is a glimpse of You.

Chorus 1

    B   F#m
All I need is You.

    A   E   B
  All I need is You, Lord, is You, ___ Lord.

      F#m
All I need is You.

    A   E   B
  All I need is You, Lord, is You, ___ Lord.

Verse 2

C#m   F#m
One more day, and it's not the same

  A   B
Your Spirit calls my heart to sing.

C#m   E   Bsus4 B
Drawn to the voice of my Savior once again.

C#m   F#m
Where would my soul be with - out Your Son?

 A   B
He gave His life to save the earth.

 C#m   E   Bsus4
I rest in the thought that You're watching over me.

Chorus 2

 B F#m
‖: All I need is You.

A   E   B
 All I need is You, Lord, is You, ___ Lord. :‖ *Play 3 times*

    F#m
All I need is You.

A   E   B
 All I need is You, Lord, is You.

Bridge 1

    F#m A
‖: All I need ___ is You.

    E B
All I need ___ is You. :‖

Chorus 3   *Repeat Chorus 1*

Interlude   ‖: A   E |B   :‖

                      A   E   B   F#m
Bridge 2   ‖: You hold   the universe.

                    A   E   B   F#m
           You hold   ev'ryone ___ on earth.

                    A   E   B   F#m
           You hold   the universe.

                    A   E   B F#m
           You hold,   You hold.   :‖

                    A   E   B   F#m
           You hold   the universe.

                    A   E   B   F#m
           You hold   ev'ryone ___ on earth.

                    A   E   B   F#m
           You hold   the universe.

                    A   E   B
           You hold,   You hold.

                         F#m
Chorus 4   ‖: All I need is You.

           A   E   B
           All I need is You, Lord, is You, ___ Lord. :‖ *Play 5 times*

                    F#m A
           All I need is You.

Break Free

Words and Music by Matt Crocker,
Joel Houston and Scott Ligertwood

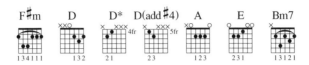

Would you be-lieve _ me, would you lis-ten if I told

F#m   D   D*   D(add#4)   A   E   Bm7

Intro

‖: N.C.(F#m) | | (D) | :‖

Verse 1

N.C.(F#m)   (D)
Would you believe me, would you listen if I told you ___ that

(F#m)   (D)
There is a love that makes a way and never holds you ___ back.

Pre-Chorus 1

N.C.(F#m)
So won't you break free, won't you break free,

          D*   D(add#4) D* D(add#4) N.C.
Get up and dance ___ in His ___ love.

(F#m)
Won't you break free, won't you break free,

          D*   D(add#4) D* D(add#4)
Get up and dance ___ in His ___ love.

Verse 2

N.C.(F#m)
Who would have thought that God

                              (D)
Would give His one and only ___ Son?

(F#m)   (D)
Taking a stand upon the cross to show us perfect ___ love.

Pre-Chorus 2

N.C.(F#m)
So won't you break free, won't you break free,

                    D*   D(add#4) D* D(add#4) N.C.
Get up and dance ___ in His ___ love.

(F#m)
So won't you break free, won't you break free,

                  D
Get up and dance ___ in His love, His love never ending.

Chorus 1

A   D
  There's no escaping the truth,

                    F#m
There's no mistaking it's You.

              D
God forever, we'll get up and dance,

Get up and dance and praise You.

A   D
  There's no escaping Your light,

                    F#m
There's no mistaking Your life.

                D
Across the world we will get up and dance,

Get up and dance and praise You.

Interlude
   | N.C.(F#m) | | (D) | |

Verse 3
N.C.(F#m)   (D)
Now is the time to take this freedom that has come our ___ way.

(F#m)   (D)
Offer our lives to see the glory of His ___ name.

Pre-Chorus 3   *Repeat Pre-Chorus 1*

Chorus 2   *Repeat Chorus 1*

Bridge
          E   F#m   D
And for all our days ___ we are holding on,

                    E   F#m   D
Holding on to all Your ways ___ we are holding on,

                    E   F#m   D
Holding on to all You said ___ and You've ___ done.

          E   F#m   D
We are holding on ___ to Your ___ love.

                    F#m   Bm7 F#m Bm7
Now we will ___ dance.

Pre-Chorus 4
          F#m
‖: So won't you break free, won't you break free,

                    Bm7
Get up and dance, ___ won't you break free. :‖ *Play 3 times*

          F#m
So won't you break free, won't you break free,

                    Bm7   D**
Get up and dance ___ in Your love, love never ending.

Chorus 3   *Repeat Chorus 1*

Outro | N.C.(F#m) | | (D) | ‖

Always

Words and Music by
Mia Fieldes

Melody:

Did You   rise the sun __ for me? __

Bm7   G   D   A/C#   A   D/F#   C   G/B

Intro

‖: Bm7 | G | D | A/C#   :‖

Verse 1

        Bm7
Did You rise the sun for me,

      G   **D**   **A/C#**
Or paint a million stars that I might know Your majesty?

        Bm7
Is Your voice upon the wind?

      G   **D**   **A/C#**
Is ev'rything I know marked with my Maker's fingerprints?

Pre-Chorus 1

G   **Bm7**   **A**   **D**
  Breathe on me, ___ let me see ___ Your face.

G   **A**
  Ever I ___ will seek You.

Chorus 1

D   **A/C#**   **Bm7**   **G**
  'Cause all You are ___ is all I want, ___ always.

D/F#   **A**   **Bm7**
  Draw me close ___ in Your arms.

        G   **D**   **A/C#** **Bm7** **G**
Oh, God, ___ I wanna be with You.

Verse 2

        Bm7
Can I feel You in the rain?

      G   **D**   **A/C#**
A - bandon all I am to have You capture me again.

        Bm7
Let the earth resound with praise.

      G   **D**   **A/C#**
Can You hear as all creation lives to glorify one Name?   Jesus.

GUITAR CHORD SONGBOOK

Pre-Chorus 2   *Repeat Pre-Chorus 1*

Chorus 2

      D   A/C♯   Bm7   G
‖: 'Cause all You are ___ is all I want, ___ always.

D/F♯   A   Bm7
   Draw me close ___ in Your arms.

        G   D
O God, ___ I wanna be with You.   :‖

Bridge

C   G/B   G
  I wanna be with You, ___ O God,

               D
I wanna be with You.

C   G/B G
  I wanna be with You.

    A   Bm7   D/F♯
Je - sus, it's all I wanna do is just be with You.

  G   A   Bm7 D/F♯
I love You, Lord. I love You, Lord.

  G   A   Bm7 D/F♯
‖: Ever I ___ will seek You.   :‖ *Play 3 times*

G   A
Ever I ___ will seek You.

Chorus 3   *Repeat Chorus 2*

Outro

C   G/B   G
  I wanna be with You, ___ O God,

               D
I wanna be with You.

C   G/B
  I wanna be with You.

| G | A | Bm7 | D/F♯ | |
| G | A | D | ‖ |

Am I To Believe

Words and Music by
Joel Houston

Melody:

Am I to be-lieve _ that a God

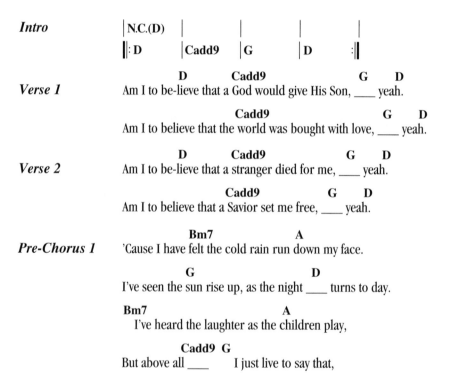

D Cadd9 G Bm7 A E Em7

Intro

| N.C.(D) | | | | |

‖: D | Cadd9 | G | D :‖

                D   **Cadd9**   **G** **D**

Verse 1   Am I to be-lieve that a God would give His Son, ____ yeah.

                              Cadd9   **G** **D**

    Am I to believe that the world was bought with love, ____ yeah.

                D   **Cadd9**   **G** **D**

Verse 2   Am I to be-lieve that a stranger died for me, ____ yeah.

                       Cadd9   **G** **D**

    Am I to believe that a Savior set me free, ____ yeah.

              Bm7   **A**

Pre-Chorus 1 'Cause I have felt the cold rain run down my face.

          G   **D**

    I've seen the sun rise up, as the night ____ turns to day.

Bm7   **A**

    I've heard the laughter as the children play,

          Cadd9 G

    But above all ____   I just live to say that,

Chorus 1

```
A        E                          Bm7      D
Yeah, oh yeah, I believe in the God ____ of love.

A        E                  G     D   Cadd9  G  D
Yeah, oh yeah, I believe in the ris - en Son.
```

Verse 3

```
            D            Cadd9           G      D
Am I to be-lieve that the sick shall overcome, ____ yeah.

                  Cadd9              G     D
Am I to believe my freedom has been won, ____ yeah.
```

Pre-Chorus 2   *Repeat Pre-Chorus 1*

Chorus 2

```
A        E                          Bm7      D
Yeah, oh yeah, I believe in the God ____ of love.

A        E                  G     D
Yeah, oh yeah, I believe in the ris - en Son.

A        E                          Bm7      D
Yeah, oh yeah, I believe in the God ____ of love.

A        Em7                G     D
Yeah, oh yeah, I believe in the ris - en Son.
```

Guitar Solo

```
‖: A      | G        | D        | A       :‖
```

Chorus 3

```
A
Yeah, oh yeah, I believe in the God of love.

                            G     D
Yeah, oh yeah, I believe in the ris - en Son.

  A        E                          Bm7      D
‖: Yeah, oh yeah, I believe in the God ____ of love.

A        Em7                G     D
Yeah, oh yeah, I believe in the ris - en Son.  :‖
```

Outro

```
‖: N.C.(D) |          |          :‖  Play 3 times
```

Came To My Rescue

Words and Music by Marty Sampson,
Dylan Thomas and Joel Davies

Melody:

Fall-ing on ___ my ___ knees ___ in ___ wor - ship,

(Capo 5th fret)

G Dsus4 D Em7 Cadd9 D/F# Em9 Gmaj7 A7sus4

Intro

| G | Dsus4 D | Em7 | Cadd9 |
| G | D/F# | Em7 | Cadd9 |

Verse 1

    G   Dsus4 D
Falling on my knees ___ in worship,

Em7   Cadd9   G
Giving all I am ___ to seek Your face.

        D/F#   Em7 Cadd9
Lord, all ___ I am is Yours.

Verse 2

    G   Dsus4 D
My whole life I place ___ in Your hands.

Em7   Cadd9   G
God of mercy, hum - bled, I bow down.

        D/F#   Em7 Cadd9
In Your pres - ence, at Your throne.

Chorus 1

      G   D/F# Em7
I called, You an - swered

      Cadd9
And You came to my rescue.

      G   D/F#   Em7 Cadd9
And I ___ wanna be where ___ You are.

Interlude 1　　　　|G　　　　　|Dsus4　D　|Em7　　　|Cadd9　　|

Verse 3　　　　　*Repeat Verse 2*

Chorus 2　　　　*Repeat Chorus 1 (Play 2 times)*

Interlude 2　　　|Em7 Em9 |Em7 D/F♯|G Gmaj7 |G A7sus4 |
　　　　　　　　　|Em7 Em9 |Em7 D　|Eadd9　|　　Dsus4|

　　　　　　　　Em7　　Em9　Em7　　D/F♯
Bridge　　　‖: In my life,　　be lifted ___ high.

　　　　　　　G　　　Gmaj7 G　　A7sus4
　　　　　　　　In our world,　be lifted ___ high.

　　　　　　　Em7　　Em9 Em7　D　　Cadd9
　　　　　　　　In our love,　be lifted high.　:‖ *Play 3 times*

　　　　　　　G　　　D/F♯　Em7
Chorus 3　　I called, You an - swered

　　　　　　　　Cadd9
　　　　　　And You came to my rescue.

　　　　　　　G　　　　　　　D/F♯　Em7 Cadd9 G
　　　　　　And I ___ wanna be where ___ You are.

Deeper

Words and Music by
Marty Sampson

Melody:

Light of men, __ love __ of God,

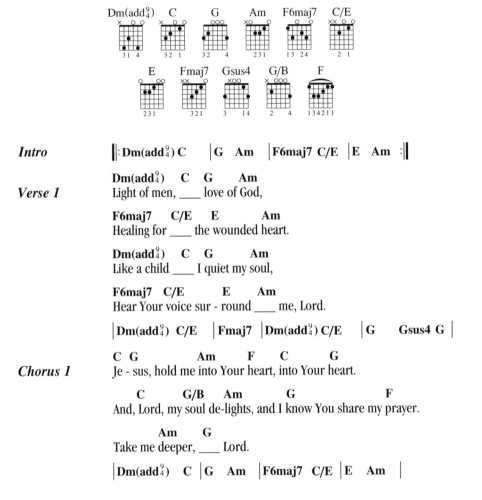

Dm(add$^9_4$) C G Am F6maj7 C/E
E Fmaj7 Gsus4 G/B F

Intro

‖: Dm(add$^9_4$) C | G Am | F6maj7 C/E | E Am :‖

Verse 1

Dm(add$^9_4$) C G Am
Light of men, ___ love of God,

F6maj7 C/E E Am
Healing for ___ the wounded heart.

Dm(add$^9_4$) C G Am
Like a child ___ I quiet my soul,

F6maj7 C/E E Am
Hear Your voice sur - round ___ me, Lord.

| Dm(add$^9_4$) C/E | Fmaj7 | Dm(add$^9_4$) C/E | G Gsus4 G |

Chorus 1

C G Am F C G
Je - sus, hold me into Your heart, into Your heart.

C G/B Am G F
And, Lord, my soul de-lights, and I know You share my prayer.

Am G
Take me deeper, ___ Lord.

| Dm(add$^9_4$) C | G Am | F6maj7 C/E | E Am |

Verse 2

Dm(add$_4^9$)   **C**   **G**   **Am**
Glorious Son, ___ to You I shall bow.

F6maj7   **C/E E**   **Am**
Bow my knee, ___ bow my will.

Dm(add$_4^9$)   **C**   **G**   **Am**
Cherished by ___ the strong and the weak.

F6maj7   **C/E**   **E**   **Am**
Humble hearts ___ shall hear ___ You speak.

| **Dm(add$_4^9$) C/E** | **Fmaj7** | **Dm(add$_4^9$) C/E** | **G**   **Gsus4 G** |

Chorus 2

C G   **Am**   **F**   **C**   **G**
Je - sus, hold me into Your heart, into Your heart.

      C   **G/B Am**   **G**   **F**
And, Lord, my soul de-lights and I know You share my prayer.

         Am G
Take me deeper.

Chorus 3

C G   **Am**   **F**   **C**   **G**
Je - sus, hold me into Your heart, into Your heart.

      C   **G/B Am**   **G**   **F**
And, Lord, my soul de-lights and I know You share my prayer.

         Am   **G**
Take me deeper, ___ Lord.

| *Interlude* | ‖: F   C | G   C | F   C | G   Gsus4 G :‖ |

Bridge

    F   C   G   C
‖: By Your love, Lord, You opened my heart,

          F   C   Gsus4
Now Your light will shine al - ways.

F   C   G   C
By Your Word, ___ Lord, Your promise secure,

       F   C   G
And my soul will live ___ al - ways.   :‖

Chorus 4   *Repeat Chorus 2*

Chorus 5   *Repeat Chorus 3*

Outro

F   Am   G
 Take me deeper, ___ Lord.

F   Am   G
 Take me deeper, ___ Lord.

| F   C | G   C | F   C | G   Gsus4 G |
| F   C | G   C | F   C | G   ‖

Desperate People

Words and Music by
Michael Guy Chislett
and Joel Houston

You crossed the great di - vide, You took _ our place. _

Fmaj7   Am   C   G   Dm   G/B   Am(add9)

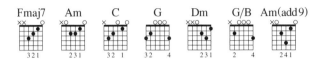

Intro

‖: **Fmaj7** | **Am**   :‖ *Play 5 times*
| **C** | **G** |

Verse 1

Fmaj7   Am
   You crossed the great di - vide, You took our place.

Fmaj7   Am
   You offered up Your life though we had failed.

Fmaj7   Am
   The veil was torn and love remained.

      C   G
You are holy, Lord.

Verse 2

Fmaj7   Am
   Distraction cast a - side, we seek Your face.

Fmaj7   Am
   We offer up our lives to bring You praise.

Fmaj7   Am
   A love that walls can - not contain.

      C   G
You are holy, Lord.

Pre-Chorus 1

       Dm   **Am**
We're rising up in spirit and in truth.

     Fmaj7   **C**
A living sacri - fice, we worship You.

      Dm   **Am**
A people undi - vided, Lord, hear us ___ sing.

     Fmaj7
We are Yours ___ and You are our King.

Chorus 1

      C   **G**
This is our ___ love, hearts joined as one.

Am   **Fmaj7**
Desperate for all You are.

         C   **G**
Lord, break down these ___ walls, and see how we run,

Dm   **Fmaj7**
Desperate for all You want. We chase Your heart.

Interlude

‖:**Fmaj7** |**Am**   :‖

Verse 3

Fmaj7   **Am**
 We didn't come to leave here entertained.

Fmaj7   **Am**
 Or worship under any other name.

Fmaj7   **Am**
 We're crying out for You alone.

    C **G**
You are holy, Lord.

Pre-Chorus 2   *Repeat Pre-Chorus 1*

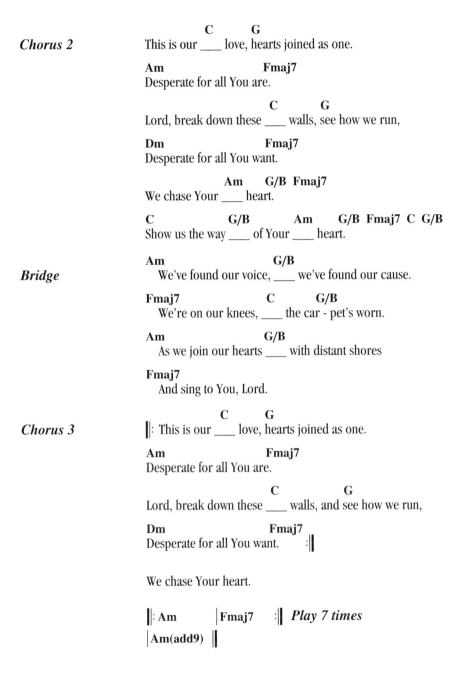

Chorus 2

           C   G
This is our ___ love, hearts joined as one.

Am   Fmaj7
Desperate for all You are.

                   C   G
Lord, break down these ___ walls, see how we run,

Dm   Fmaj7
Desperate for all You want.

              Am   G/B Fmaj7
We chase Your ___ heart.

C   G/B   Am   G/B Fmaj7 C G/B
Show us the way ___ of Your ___ heart.

Bridge

Am   G/B
  We've found our voice, ___ we've found our cause.

Fmaj7   C   G/B
  We're on our knees, ___ the car - pet's worn.

Am   G/B
  As we join our hearts ___ with distant shores

Fmaj7
  And sing to You, Lord.

Chorus 3

           C   G
‖: This is our ___ love, hearts joined as one.

Am   Fmaj7
Desperate for all You are.

                   C   G
Lord, break down these ___ walls, and see how we run,

Dm   Fmaj7
Desperate for all You want.   :‖

We chase Your heart.

‖: Am |Fmaj7   :‖ *Play 7 times*
|Am(add9) ‖

Evermore

Words and Music by
Joel Houston

Melody:

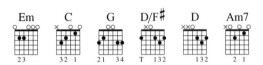

We're lost for words, with all   to ____ say,

Em   C   G   D/F#   D   Am7

Intro   ‖: Em | C | G | D/F# :‖

Verse 1
        Em   **C**
We're lost for words, with all to ___ say,

    G   **D/F#**
Lord, You take my breath a - way.

      Em   **C**
Still my soul, my soul cries ___ out,

       G **D/F#**
For You are ho - ly.

Verse 2
        Em   **C**
And as I look upon Your ___ name

    G   **D/F#**
Circum - stances fade a - way.

      Em   **C**
Now Your glory steals my ___ heart,

      G **D/F#**
For You are ho - ly.

     Em D/F# C   **Em**   **D/F# C**
You are holy,   You are ho - ly, Lord.

We'll say,

Chorus 1	G D
	Evermore my heart, my heart will say,
	C Em D
	Above all ____ I live for Your glory.
	G D
	And even if my world falls I will say,
	C Em D
	Above all ____ I live for Your glory.
	I live for Your glory.

| *Interlude* | \|Em   \|C   \|G   \|D/F♯   \| |

| *Verse 3* | *Repeat Verse 1* |

| *Verse 4* | *Repeat Verse 2* |

| *Chorus 2* | *Repeat Chorus 1* |

Bridge	C Em D
	Oh, Je - sus, I live for Your glory.
	C Em D
	Lord, ____ and I'll be there ____ with all my heart.
	Am7 C G
	I'll say ____ I'm liv - ing for Your name.
	D/F♯ Am7
	With all ____ to give You praise.
	C G D/F♯
	We're liv - ing for Your glo - ry, Lord.

| *Chorus 3* | *Repeat Chorus 1* |

| *Chorus 4* | *Repeat Chorus 2* |

| *Outro* | C   Em   D |
| | \|: Above all ____ I live ____ for Your glory. :\| |

Everyday

Words and Music by
Joel Houston

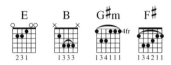

E   B   G#m   F#

Intro   ‖: E   B |G#m   F#   :‖

Verse 1
    E   B   G#m   F#
    What to say, Lord? It's ____ You who gave ____ me life.

       E   B   G#m   F#
And I ____ can't explain ____ just how ____ much You mean ____ to me.

       E   B   G#m
Now ____ that You have saved ____ me, Lord,

           F#   E
I give all that ____ I am to You

           B   G#m   F#
That ev'ry day ____ I can ____be a light ____ that shines Your name.

Interlude 1   ‖: E   B |G#m F# :‖

Verse 2
    E   B   G#m   F#
    Ev'ry day, ____ Lord, I'll ____ learn to stand ____ upon Your word.

    E   B   G#m   F#
    And I pray ____ that I, ____ that I might come ____ to know You more.

    E   B   G#m   F#
    That You would guide ____ me in ev'ry single step ____ I take.

       E   B   G#m   F#   B
That ____ ev'ry day ____ I can ____ be Your light ____ unto the world.

Chorus 1

         E   G#m F# B
Ev'ry day, ___ it's You I'll live for.

         E   G#m F# B
Ev'ry day, ___ I'll follow after You.

         E   G#m   F#   B E G#m7 F#
Ev'ry day, ___ I'll walk with You, my Lord.

Interlude 2 ‖: E B │G#m F# :‖

Verse 3   *Repeat Verse 2*

Chorus 2   *Repeat Chorus 1*

Chorus 3

B   E   G#m F# B
  Ev'ry day, ___ it's You I'll live for.

         E   G#m F# B
Ev'ry day, ___ I'll follow after You.

         E   G#m   F#   B E G#m F#
Ev'ry day, ___ I'll walk with You, my Lord.

Chorus 4

    B   E   G#m   F#
‖: It's You I live ___ for ev - 'ry day.

    B   E   G#m   F#
It's You I live ___ for ev - 'ry day.

    B   E   G#m   F# B E G#m F#
It's You I live ___ for ev - 'ry day.   :‖ *Play 3 times*

    B   E   G#m   F#
‖: It's You I live ___ for ev - 'ry day. :‖

    B
It's You I live for ev'ry day.

Everything To Me

Words and Music by
Marty Sampson

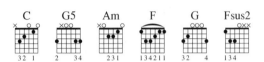

C   G5   Am   F   G   Fsus2

32 1	2 34	231	134211	32 4	134

Intro   ‖: C | G5 | Am | F   :‖

                    C   N.C.(G)

Verse 1   Jesus Christ, King of glory.

            (F) (C) (G)
            Lord of all, we praise You.

            Am   F   C   G5
            For - ever Your name ___ will ___ be praised

            Am F   C   G
            In heaven and earth ___ always.

Interlude | C | G5 | Am | F |

                    C   N.C.(G)

Verse 2   Jesus Christ, You're my Saviour.

             (F) (C) (G)
            And I will run af - ter You.

            Am   F   C   G5
            For You are the Son ___ of God

                Am F   C   G5
            And   King over all ___ the world.

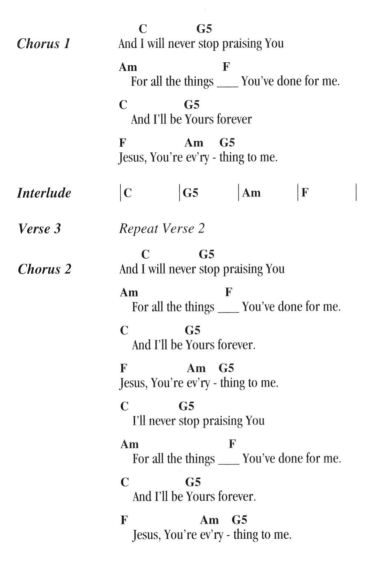

Chorus 1

C   G5
And I will never stop praising You

Am   F
For all the things ____ You've done for me.

C   G5
And I'll be Yours forever

F   Am G5
Jesus, You're ev'ry - thing to me.

Interlude

| C | G5 | Am | F |

Verse 3   *Repeat Verse 2*

Chorus 2

C   G5
And I will never stop praising You

Am   F
For all the things ____ You've done for me.

C   G5
And I'll be Yours forever.

F   Am G5
Jesus, You're ev'ry - thing to me.

C   G5
I'll never stop praising You

Am   F
For all the things ____ You've done for me.

C   G5
And I'll be Yours forever.

F   Am G5
Jesus, You're ev'ry - thing to me.

Bridge

     C   G5
‖:   Jesus, You're ev'rything to me.

Am   F
Jesus, You're ev'rything to me. :‖ *Play 3 times*

C   G5
Jesus, You're ev'rything to me.

Am   F
Jesus, You're ev'rything.

Chorus 3

     C   G5
And I will never stop praising You

Am   F
For all the things ____ You've done for me.

C   G5
And I'll be Yours forever.

F   Am   G5
Jesus, You're ev'ry - thing to me.

C   G5
I'll never stop praising You

Am   F
For all the things ____ You've done for me.

C   G5
And I'll be Yours forever.

F   Am   G5
Jesus, You're ev'ry - thing to me.

Outro

     C   G5
‖:   Jesus, You're ev'rything to me.

Am   F
Jesus, You're ev'rything to me.   :‖

Am   Fsus2
Jesus.

God Is Great

Words and Music by
Marty Sampson

Melody:

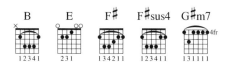

All __ cre - a - tion cries __ to You, __

B   E   F#   F#sus4   G#m7

1 2 3 4 1   2 3 1   1 3 4 2 1 1   1 2 3 4 1 1   1 3 1 1 1

Intro   ‖: B |E |F# |E   :‖

Verse 1

B   E   F#sus4 F#
All crea - tion cries to You,

B   E   F#sus4 F#
Worshiping in Spir - it and in truth.

G#m7   E   F#sus4
Glory to ____ the Faithful One,

G#m7 F#   E F# E F#
Jesus   Christ, God's Son.

Verse 2

B   E   F#sus4 F#
All crea - tion gives You praise,

B   E   F#sus4 F#
You alone ____ are truly great.

G#m7   E   F#
You alone ____ are God who reigns

G#m7 F#   E F# E F#
For e - terni - ty.

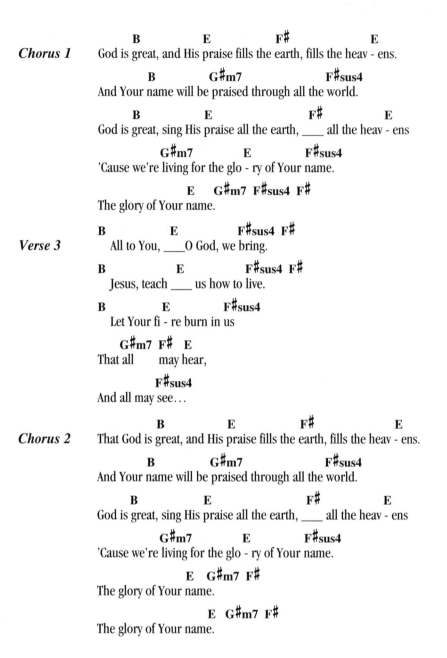

Chorus 1

          B   E   F#   E
God is great, and His praise fills the earth, fills the heav - ens.

              B   G#m7   F#sus4
And Your name will be praised through all the world.

          B   E   F#   E
God is great, sing His praise all the earth, ____ all the heav - ens

            G#m7   E   F#sus4
'Cause we're living for the glo - ry of Your name.

                        E   G#m7 F#sus4 F#
The glory of Your name.

Verse 3

          B   E   F#sus4 F#
    All to You, ____O God, we bring.

      B   E   F#sus4 F#
    Jesus, teach ____ us how to live.

      B   E   F#sus4
    Let Your fi - re burn in us

      G#m7 F#   E
That all   may hear,

          F#sus4
And all may see…

Chorus 2

              B   E   F#   E
That God is great, and His praise fills the earth, fills the heav - ens.

              B   G#m7   F#sus4
And Your name will be praised through all the world.

          B   E   F#   E
God is great, sing His praise all the earth, ____ all the heav - ens

            G#m7   E   F#sus4
'Cause we're living for the glo - ry of Your name.

                    E   G#m7 F#
The glory of Your name.

                        E   G#m7 F#
The glory of Your name.

Bridge

B   E   F#sus4   F#   G#m7
‖: Holy is the Lord,   the whole earth sings,

E   F#sus4   F#
   The whole earth sings.   :‖ *Play 4 times*

Chorus 3

     B   E   F#   E
God is great, and His praise fills the earth, fills the heav - ens.

     B   G#m7   F#sus4
And Your name will be praised through all the world.

     B   E   F#   E
God is great, sing His praise all the earth, ___ all the heav - ens

     G#m7   E   F#sus4
'Cause we're living for the glo - ry of Your name.

     G#m7   E   F#sus4
'Cause we're living for the glo - ry of Your name.

     B   E   F#sus4
The glory of Your name.

     B   E   F#sus4   E   B
The glory of Your name.

Fire Fall Down

Words and Music by
Matt Crocker

Melody: 'Cause I know ___ that You're a-live.

(Capo 2nd fret)

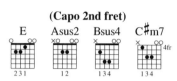

E   Asus2   Bsus4   C#m7

Intro
‖: E |Asus2   :‖ *Play 3 times*

Chorus 1
                        E   Asus2
'Cause I know ____ that You're a - live.

                        E   Asus2
You came to fix ____ my broken life.

                    E   Asus2   E   Asus2
And I sing ____ to glori - fy Your Holy name, ____ Jesus ____ Christ.

Interlude 1
|E |Asus2 |E |Asus2 |

Verse 1
E   Asus2
    You bought my life with the blood that you shed on the cross.

                                                    Bsus4
When You died for the sins of men, and You let ____ out a cry.

                            E
Crucified, now alive in me.

Verse 2
E   Asus2
    These hands are Yours, teach them to serve as You please.

                                        Bsus4
And I'll reach out, desperate to see all the great - ness of God.

                            E
May my soul rest assured in You.

Pre-Chorus 1

Asus2   Bsus4
I'll never be the same,

Asus2   Bsus4
No, I'll never be the same.

Chorus 2   *Repeat Chorus 1*

Interlude 2 | E | |

Verse 3

E
You've changed it all, You broke down the wall.

          Asus2
When I spoke ___ and confessed, in You I am blessed.

       Bsus4   E
Now I walk ___ in the light, in victorious sight of You.

Pre-Chorus 2   *Repeat Pre-Chorus 1*

Chorus 3

          E   Asus2
‖: 'Cause I know ___ that You're a - live.

          E   Asus2
You came to fix ___ my broken life.

         E   Asus2   C#m7   Asus2
And I sing ___ to glori - fy Your Holy name, Jesus ___ Christ. :‖

Interlude 3 | E | | | |

Bridge

     E   Asus2
‖: Your fire fall down, ___ Your fire fall down

C#m7   Asus2
On us we pray ___ as we seek. :‖ *Play 8 times*

Outro

     E   Asus2
‖: Show me Your heart, ___ show me Your way,

C#m7   Asus2
Show me Your glo - ry. :‖ *Play 8 times*

| E   ‖

Forever

Words and Music by
Marty Sampson

Melody:

I'll wor-ship at Your throne, whis-per my own love song. __

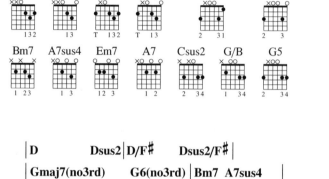

D Dsus2 D/F♯ Dsus2/F♯ Gmaj7(no3rd) G6(no3rd)

Bm7 A7sus4 Em7 A7 Csus2 G/B G5

Intro

| D   Dsus2 | D/F♯ Dsus2/F♯ |
| Gmaj7(no3rd) G6(no3rd) | Bm7 A7sus4 |

Verse 1

D   Dsus2 D/F♯   Dsus2/F♯
I'll worship at Your throne, whisper my own love song.

Gmaj7(no3rd) G6(no3rd) Bm7   A7sus4
With all my heart I'll sing   for You, my Dad and King.

D   Dsus2 D/F♯   Dsus2/F♯
I'll live for all my days to put a smile on Your face.

Gmaj7(no3rd) G6(no3rd) Bm7   A7sus4
And when we finally meet   it'll be for e - ternity.

Pre-Chorus 1

    Em7   Bm7
And oh, ____ how wide

    A7sus4   A7
You open up ____ Your arms when I need Your love.

Em7 Bm7   A7sus4 A7
And how far You would come ____ if ever I was lost.

Csus2 G/B   A7sus4   A7
You said that all You feel ____ for me is undying love

Csus2   Em7 D/F♯ G5 A7sus4
That You showed me through the cross.

Chorus 1

D
I'll worship You, my God.

Dsus2/F#
I'll worship You, my God.

G5   Bm7   A7sus4
I love You,   I love You.

D   Dsus2/F#   G5
Forever I will sing,   forever I will be ___ with You,

  Bm7   A7
Be ___ with You.

Interlude 1 | D | Dsus2/F# | G5 | Bm7 A7 |

Verse 2

D   Dsus2/F#
I'll worship at Your throne,   whisper my own love song.

G5   Bm7   A7sus4
With all my heart I'll sing   for You, my Dad and King.

D   Dsus2/F#
I'll live for all my days   to put a smile on Your face.

Gmaj7(no3rd)   Bm7   A7sus4
And when we finally meet   it'll be for e - ternity.

Pre-Chorus 2   *Repeat Pre-Chorus 1*

Chorus 2   *Repeat Chorus 1*

Chorus 3   *Repeat Chorus 1*

Interlude 2 ||: D | Dsus2/F# | G5 | Bm7 A7 :||

Pre-Chorus 3   *Repeat Pre-Chorus 1*

Chorus 4   *Repeat Chorus 1*

Chorus 5   *Repeat Chorus 1*

Outro | D | D/F# | G5 | Bm7 A7sus4 | D ||

Found

Words and Music by
Dave George

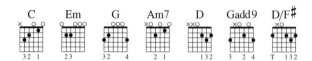

C   Em   G   Am7   D   Gadd9   D/F#

Intro

‖: C Em |G Am7 |C   Em |G C :‖

Verse 1

    C   Em   G
    Amaz - ing love,

           Am7   C   Em G C
Now what ____ else shall I need?

            Em   G
Your name ____ brings life,

       Am7   C   Em G C
More ____ than the air I breathe.

Interlude 1

|C Em |G Am7 |C   Em |G   C |

Verse 2

    C   Em   G
    My world ____ was changed

           Am7   C   Em G C
When Your ____ life You gave for me.

        Em   G
My pur - pose found,

         Am7   C   Em G C
And all ____ that You want for me.

Chorus 1
    D   Em   C   Gadd9 D/F#
And I've found ___ myself ___ in You.

                  Em   C
And I've found ___ myself ___ in You.

Interlude 2   *Repeat Interlude 1*

Verse 3   *Repeat Verse 1*

Chorus 2
    D   Em   C   Gadd9 D/F#
And I've found ___ myself ___ in You.

                  Em   C   G   D/F#
And I've found ___ myself ___ in You.

                  Em   C   Gadd9 D/F#
And I've found ___ myself ___ in You.

                  Em   C   G
And I've found ___ myself ___ in You.

Bridge
    D   C   G   D   C
So take me to a place ___ where I can see ___ You face ___ to face.

              Em   D   Am7
All I wanna do, ___ all I wanna do ___ is worship You.

                    C   G   D   C
And take me to a place ___ where I can see ___ You face ___ to face.

              Em   D   Am7 C
All I wanna do, ___ all I wanna do ___ is worship You.

           G   D   Am7 C
Yeah, yeah, ___ yeah, yeah. ___ Worship You.

           G   D
And I'll wor - ship You, I'll wor - ship.

    Am7   C   G   D
‖: I will live for all ___ my days to wor - ship You. :‖

Chorus 3   *Repeat Chorus 2*

Free

Words and Music by
Marty Sampson

Melody:

Would you be - lieve me __ if I __ said

(Capo 4th fret)

| | C | G | G/B | D | Am | Em | F |

Verse 1

                                C   G   G/B   C
Would you be - lieve me if I ____ said that we are the ones
        G   C   G/B   D
Who can make the change ____ in the world today?
                          C   G   G/B   C
Would you be - lieve me if I ____ said that all of the dreams
        D   C   D
In your heart can come true ____ today?
                          C   G   G/B   C
Would you be - lieve me if I ____ said that life could be all
        D   C   G/B D   C   N.C.
That you want it to be today?

Chorus 1

                       C   G
And if I had wings I would fly,
                   D
'Cause all that I need You are.
                  C   Am
And if the world caved in around ____ me,
        Em   D
To You I'd still hold on.
             Am
'Cause You're all that I believe,
         F
And the One that created me.
Am   C   G C   Am   Em
Jesus, because of You I'm free.
| G   C | Am   C |

Verse 2

```
                    C              G
And would you be - lieve me if I ____ said
        G/B        C       D          C  G/B  D
That God can make miracles happen today?
                  C            G
Would you be - lieve me if I ____ said
          G/B        C        D
That you don't need to wait for the answers
        C              D
Be - fore you step out in faith?
                  C            G
Would you be - lieve me if I ____ said
        G/B       C      D       C      G/B  D  C  N.C.
That nothing is ever im - possible ____ for God?
```

Chorus 2

Repeat Chorus 1

Bridge

```
C  N.C.              G  N.C.           Em
   Just live your life ____ with God inside.
N.C.              D  N.C.            C  N.C.
You won't regret ____ one moment of ____ it.
                    Am          F
And give all that ____ you can for ____ God, for God.
```

Chorus 3

```
                  C              G
‖: 'Cause if I had wings I would fly,
                     D
And all that I need ____ You are.
          C                   Am
And if the world caved in around ____ me,
    Em              D
To You I'd still hold on.
                  Am
'Cause You're all that I believe,
            F
And the One that created me.
Am            C
Jesus, because of You.  :‖
```

Outro

```
        G    C  Am Em   G   C  Am C
‖: I'm free.          I'm free.        :‖
```

```
I'm free.
```

From God Above

Words and Music by
Marty Sampson

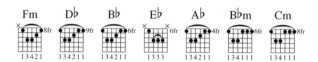

As I look at the world _ I be-gin to dream _

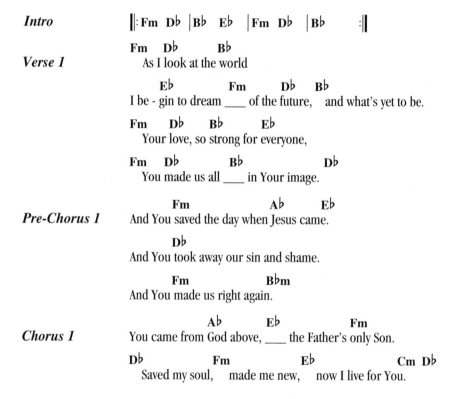

Intro ‖: Fm Db │Bb Eb │Fm Db │Bb :‖

Verse 1

Fm   Db   Bb
As I look at the world

     Eb   Fm   Db Bb
I be - gin to dream ___ of the future,   and what's yet to be.

Fm   Db   Bb   Eb
Your love, so strong for everyone,

Fm   Db   Bb   Db
You made us all ___ in Your image.

Pre-Chorus 1

         Fm   Ab   Eb
And You saved the day when Jesus came.

         Db
And You took away our sin and shame.

         Fm   Bbm
And You made us right again.

Chorus 1

         Ab   Eb   Fm
You came from God above, ___ the Father's only Son.

Db   Fm   Eb   Cm Db
Saved my soul,   made me new,   now I live for You.

Interlude 1 |Fm Db |Bb Eb |Fm Db |Bb |

Verse 2
Fm Db   Bb   Eb
My heart is a - live and my spirit free,

Fm   Db   Bb
In the Savior,   He gave His life for me.

Fm   Db   Bb   Eb
By Your Word, we will be the light of the world.

Fm Db   Bb   Db
My Father,   shine Your light in me.

Pre-Chorus 2   *Repeat Pre-Chorus 1*

Chorus 2
                    Ab   Eb   Fm
‖: You came from God above, ___ the Father's only Son.

Db   Fm   Eb   Cm Db
Saved my soul,   made me new,   now I live for You.   :‖

Interlude 2 |Ab | | | |

Bridge
Db
‖:   I'll stand on the Word, be a light in the world.

                                        Ab
When Your praises are heard, we'll be singing.   :‖

We'll be singing, we'll be singing, we'll be singing.

Chorus 3   *Repeat Chorus 2*

Outro |Fm Db |Bb Eb |Fm Db |Bb |
                                        I live for You.

|Fm Db |Bb Eb |Fm Db |Bb   ‖

From The Inside Out

Words and Music by
Joel Houston

Melody:

A thou-sand times I've ___ failed, _ still Your

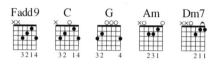

Fadd9 C G Am Dm7
3214 32 14 32 4 231 2 11

Intro	‖: **Fadd9** | C G :‖ *Play 4 times*	

Verse 1

              Fadd9   **C**   **G**
A thousand times I've failed, still Your mer - cy remains.

              Fadd9   **C**   **G**
And should I stumble again, still I'm caught ___ in Your grace.

        Am   **Fadd9**   **C**   **G**
Everlast - ing, Your light will shine when all else fades.

        Am   **Fadd9**   **C**   **G**
Neverend - ing, Your glory goes be - yond all fame.

Interlude 1   ‖: **Fadd9** \| C G :‖

Verse 2

              Fadd9   **C**   **G**
Your will a - bove all else, my pur - pose remains.

              Fadd9   **C**   **G**
The art of losing myself in bring - ing You praise.

        Am   **Fadd9**   **C**   **G**
Everlast - ing, Your light will shine when all else fades.

        Am   **Fadd9**   **C**   **G**
Neverend - ing, Your glory goes be - yond all fame.

Pre-Chorus 1

Fadd9   C
And my heart and my soul, ___ Lord, I give You control.

Am   G
Consume me from the inside out, Lord.

Fadd9   Am
And let justice and praise ___ become my embrace,

G   Dm7
To love You from the inside out.

Interlude 2   *Repeat Interlude 1*

Verse 3   *Repeat Verse 2*

Pre-Chorus 2   *Repeat Pre-Chorus 1*

Chorus 1

      Am   Fadd9   C   G
Everlast - ing, Your light ___ will shine when all else fades.

      Am   Fadd9   C   G
Neverend - ing, Your glo - ry goes be - yond all fame.

         C   Fadd9   G   Am
And the cry ___ of my heart ___ is to bring ___ You praise.

      Fadd9 G   Fadd9   G
From the in - side   out, Lord, my soul ___ cries out.

Guitar Solo

| Fadd9 | C | Am | G | |
| Fadd9 | Am | G | Dm7 | |

Pre-Chorus 3   *Repeat Pre-Chorus 1*

Chorus 2   *Repeat Chorus 1*

Chorus 3

      Am   Fadd9   C   G
Everlast - ing, Your light ___ will shine when all else fades.

      Am   Fadd9   C   G
Neverend - ing, Your glo - ry goes be - yond all fame.

         C   Fadd9   G   Am
And the cry ___ of my heart ___ is to bring ___ You praise.

      Fadd9 G   Fadd9   G
From the in - side out, Lord, my soul ___ cries out.

      Fadd9 G   Fadd9   G   Fadd9
From the in - side out, Lord, my soul ___ cries out, Lord.

Glory

Words and Music by
Reuben Morgan

Great is   the   Lord _   God

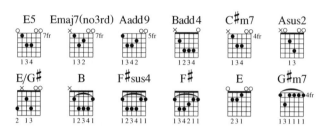

Intro	‖: **E5** | **Emaj7(no3rd)** | **Aadd9** |	:‖ *Play 4 times*

Verse 1

E5　　　　**Emaj7(no 3rd) Aadd9**
Great is the Lord God Al - mighty.

E5　　　　　**Emaj7(no 3rd) Aadd9**
Great is the Lord on　　　high.

E5　　　　　　**Emaj7(no 3rd) Aadd9**
The train of His robe fills the　　temple,

　　　Badd4 C#m7 Aadd9
And we cry out highest praise.

Pre-Chorus 1

Asus2 E/G#　C#m7 B
Glo - ry to the risen　King,

Asus2 E/G#　F#sus4 F#
Glo - ry to the Son,

　　　Aadd9
Glorious ____ Son.

Chorus 1

E
Lift up your heads, open the doors.

C#m7
Let the King ____ of glory come in,

Aadd9 C#m7 Badd4 B
And for - ever   be our God.

Interlude

| E | | | |

Verse 2

E5   Emaj7(no 3rd) Aadd9
Holy is the Lord God Al - mighty.

E5   Emaj7(no 3rd) Aadd9
Holy is the Lord on   high.

E5   Emaj7(no 3rd)   Aadd9
Let all the earth of bow be - fore You,

Badd 4   C#m7 Aadd9
And crown You Lord of all.

Pre-Chorus 2   *Repeat Pre-Chorus 1*

Chorus 2   *Repeat Chorus 1*

Chorus 3   *Repeat Chorus 1*

Guitar Solo

||: G#m7 | | Aadd9 | |
| C#m7 | | Badd4 | B   :||

Pre-Chorus 3

Asus2 E/G#   C#m7 B
Glo - ry to the risen   King,

Asus2 E/G#   F#sus4 F#
Glo - ry to the Son,

Aadd9
Glorious ____ Son.

F#sus4 F#   Aadd9
||: To the Son,   glorious ____ Son. :||

Chorus 4

E
||: Lift up your heads, open the doors.

C#m7
Let the King ____ of glory come in,

Aadd9 C#m7 Badd4 B   E
And for - ever   be our God.   :||

God Is Moving

Words and Music by
Marty Sampson

Melody:

Ho - ly Spir - it, touch Your peo - ple,

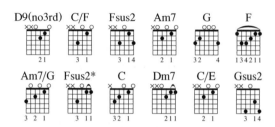

D9(no3rd) C/F Fsus2 Am7 G F

Am7/G Fsus2* C Dm7 C/E Gsus2

Intro
‖: D9(no3rd) | | C/F | Fsus2 :‖

Verse 1
D9(no3rd)   C/F   Fsus2
Holy Spirit, touch Your people, ___ teach us the ways of God.

D9(no3rd)   C/F   Fsus2
And as we live as Jesus did, You are honored and lifted up.

Pre-Chorus 1
Am7   G   F   G
There's a stirring in the Spirit, there's an urgency in this hour.

Am7   Am7/G Fsus2*
We as children must obey, can you hear the footsteps of God?

Chorus 1
                C   Dm7   C/E   F
‖: God is moving,   God is moving.

            Am7   G   Fsus2*
Can you hear the sound of re - vival?   :‖

Interlude	*Repeat Intro*

Verse 2

D9(no3rd)   **C/F**   **Fsus2**
As we praise You, as we sing,   draw near to us, O God.

D9(no3rd)   **C/F**   **Fsus2**
As we cry out for the nations, pour out revival in the land.

Pre-Chorus 2	*Repeat Pre-Chorus 1*
Chorus 2	*Repeat Chorus 1*
Chorus 3	*Repeat Chorus 1*

Interlude

‖ N.C. | ‖: | :‖ ***Play 4 times***
‖: Fsus2 | | Gsus2 | :‖ ***Play 12 times***

Pre-Chorus 3	*Repeat Pre-Chorus 1*
Chorus 4	*Repeat Chorus 1*
Chorus 5	*Repeat Chorus 1*

God Of All Creation

Words and Music by
Paul Iannuzzelli and Mark Stevens

Melody:

I'm   to-tal-ly __ a-ban - doned _ to You. __

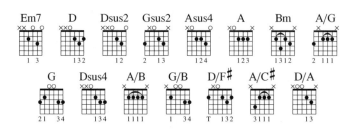

Verse 1

> N.C.   **Em7**
> I'm totally abandoned to You.
>
> **D**   **Dsus2**   **Em7**
> I'm lost inside the rivers of Your love.
>
> **Dsus2**   **Em7**
> I'm swept into the power of Your pres - ence,
>
> **Gsus2**   **Asus4**   **A**
> Drawn toward the whisper of Your ____ voice.

Verse 2

> **Dsus2**   **Em7**
> I come to You in quiet adora - tion,
>
> **Dsus2**   **Em7**
> And fall before Your feet, You are my King.
>
> **Bm7**   **Gsus2**
> I'm living for the beauty of Your pres - ence,
>
> **Em7**   **Asus4**   **A**
> To behold the glory of Your ____ face.

Chorus 1

A/G G A/G G   Dsus4 D Dsus4 D
Ho - ly, wor - thy, He is the Lord.

A/G G A/G G   Dsus4 D Dsus4 D
Heav - en de - clares Your righteousness.

  Bm7   Asus4 Gsus2 Asus4   Gsus2 Asus4 A
O God of all ___ crea - tion,   I worship You.

Verse 3   *Repeat Verse 2*

Chorus 2

A/G G A/G G   Dsus4 D Dsus4 D
Ho - ly, wor - thy, He is the Lord.

A/G   G A/G G   Dsus4 D Dsus4 D
Heav - en de - clares Your righteousness.

A/G G A/G G   Dsus4 D Dsus4 D
Ho - ly, wor - thy, He is the Lord.

A/B G/B A/B G/B   D/F♯ G Asus4
Heav - en de - clares Your righteousness.

Bm7   Asus4 Gsus2 Asus4   Gsus2 Asus4 A
God of all ___ crea - tion,   I worship You.

Bridge

  Gsus2   Aadd2/C♯   Bm7 D/A
‖: When You said seek ___ Your face,

  Gsus2   Asus4   A
My heart said Your face I will seek.   :‖

Chorus 3   *Repeat Chorus 2*

Interlude | Dsus4 D | Dsus4 D |

Chorus 4   *Repeat Chorus 2*

Outro   ‖: A/G G | A/G G | Dsus4 D | Dsus4 D   :‖

Heaven

Words and Music by
Reuben Morgan

I need _ Your _ love ___ like the des-ert

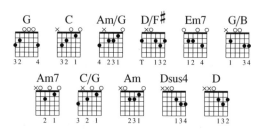

G   C   Am/G   D/F#   Em7   G/B
Am7   C/G   Am   Dsus4   D

Intro ‖: G | | C | :‖

Verse 1
G   Am/G
I need Your love, like the desert needs the rain.

G   Am/G
I need Your touch, like the fire needs the flame.

Chorus 1
D/F#   Em7   C
One moment without ____ You near

            G/B Am7 C/G   D/F#
Is heartache I can - not ____ bear.

                  Em7   C G/B
A lifetime with You, ____ oh, Lord,

    Am   Dsus4 D
Is heaven I long to know.

        C   G
Heav - en.

| C | | G | | |

Verse 2

G   Am/G
Come cover me, like the ocean meets the shore.

G   Am/G
Shine on my life, like the morning steals the nights.

Chorus 2

D/F#   Em7   C
One moment without ____ You near

G/B   Am7 C/G   D/F#
Is heartache I can - not ____ bear.

                    Em7   C G/B
A lifetime with You, ____ O Lord,

Am   C/G   D/F#
Is heaven I long ____ to know.

                    Em7   C
One moment without ____ You near

G/B   Am7 C/G   D/F#
Is heartache I can - not ____ bear.

Em7   C G/B Am7   C/G   Dsus4 D
A life - time with You,   is heaven I long ____ to know.

          C   Em7
‖: Heav - en.   :‖

Outro

‖:C | |Em7 | :‖
|C | |G | ‖

Hosanna

Words and Music by
Brooke Fraser

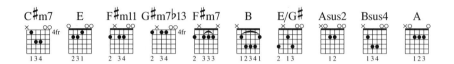

I see the King of glo - ry

C#m7   E   F#m11   G#m7♭13   F#m7   B   E/G#   Asus2   Bsus4   A

Intro   ‖: C#m7 | E | F#m11 | G#m7♭13 :‖

Verse 1
      E   C#m7
I see the King of glory coming on the clouds with fire.
                     F#m7   B C#m7
The whole earth shakes, ___ the whole earth shakes.

Verse 2
      E   C#m7
I see His love and mercy washing over all our sin.
                 F#m7   B
The people sing, ___ the people sing.

Chorus 1
         E/G# Asus2   Bsus4 C#m7
Hosan - na,   Hosan - na,
         Asus2   C#m7 Bsus4
Ho - sanna in the highest.
         E/G# Asus2   Bsus4 C#m7
Hosan - na,   Hosan - na,
         Asus2   Bsus4 C#m7
Ho - sanna in the highest.

Verse 3
      E   C#m7
I see a generation rising up to take their place.
               F#m7   B
With selfless faith, ___ with selfless faith.

Verse 4

```
E                       C#m7
I see a near revival stirring as we pray and seek.

          F#m7                    B
We're on our knees, ___ we're on our knees.
```

Chorus 2   *Repeat Chorus 1*

Interlude   *Repeat Intro*

Bridge

```
A                         B
Heal my heart and make it clean,

E                       C#m7
Open up my eyes to the things unseen.

A                         B             C#m7
Show me how to love like You ___ have loved me.

A                         B
Break my heart for what breaks Yours.

E                       C#m7
Ev'rything I am for Your kingdom's cause

A                       B         Asus2
As I walk from earth into ___ eternity.
```

Chorus 3

```
        E/G# Asus2      Bsus4 C#m7
Hosan - na,      Hosan - na,

        Asus2     C#m7 Bsus4
Ho - sanna in the highest.

        E/G# Asus2      Bsus4 C#m7
Hosan - na,      Hosan - na,

        Asus2      Bsus4 E
Ho - sanna in the highest.
```

Chorus 4   *Repeat Chorus 1*

Outro

```
        A       B    E
Ho - sanna in the highest.
```

I Adore

Words and Music by
Reuben Morgan

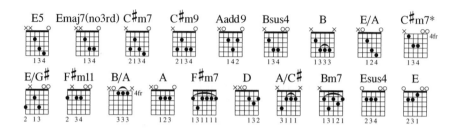

Verse 1

   E5   Emaj7(no3rd)   C#m7 C#m9
   The u - niverse is at Your feet,

         Aadd9   Bsus4 B
   Gives You praise ____ evermore.

   E5   Emaj7(no3rd)   C#m7 C#m9
   The stars will light the sky for You,

       Aadd9   Bsus4 B
   And always ____ God be praised.

Pre-Chorus 1

        E/A   Bsus4
   And we sing ____ the Lord is on high,

     C#m7* Aadd9 C#m7* Bsus4
   The Lord is on _____ high.

Chorus 1

    B   **E/G♯**   **Aadd9**
I adore ____ You,

       F♯m11 E/G♯   **Bsus4**
I adore _____ You.

         Aadd9   **E/G♯**
And there's none ___ that compares

        F♯m11 E/G♯   **B**
To Your maj - esty, ___ O Lord.

B/A   **E/G♯**   **Aadd9**
I adore _____ You,

       F♯m11 E/G♯ **Bsus4**
I adore _____ You,

       Aadd9
And I stand

      Bsus4   **E5 Emaj7(no3rd) E5 Emaj7(no3rd)**
In the won - der of Your love.

Verse 2   *Repeat Verse 1*

Pre-Chorus 2   *Repeat Pre-Chorus 1*

Chorus 2

    B   **E/G♯**   **Aadd9**
I adore ___ You,

       F♯m11 E/G♯   **Bsus4**
I adore _____ You.

         Aadd9   **E/G♯**
And there's none ___ that compares

        F♯m11 E/G♯   **B**
To Your Maj - esty, ___ O Lord.

B/A   **E/G♯**   **Aadd9**
I adore _____ You,

       F♯m11 E/G♯ **Bsus4**
I adore _____ You,

       Aadd9
And I stand

      Bsus4   **E5 Emaj7(no3rd) C♯m7 C♯m9**
In the won - der of Your love.

| **Aadd9**   **E/G♯** | **F♯m11**   **Bsus4 B** |

Bridge

E5   Emaj7(no3rd) C#m7   C#m9
We will crown Him _____ King for - ever.

A   E/G#   F#m11   Bsus4 B
Living Saviour, Jesus, Re - deem - er.

E5   Emaj7(no3rd) C#m7   C#m9
Lord of Heaven,   robed in majesty.

A   E/G#   F#m11   Bsus4 B
Crowned in glory, cre - ation adores _____ You.

Outro

A   F#m7
Holy, holy,   God Almighty.

D   A/C# Bm7   Esus4 E
And for - ever the Lord is ex - alt - ed.

A   F#m7
Hear the angels   shout His anthems.

D   A/C# Bm7   Esus4 E A E/G# F#m7 E
||: Ever - living God, we a - dore You.   :||

D   A/C# Bm7   Esus4   E
Ever - living God, we a - dore You.

My Future Decided

Words and Music by Marty Sampson,
Joel Houston and Jonathon Douglass

Melody:

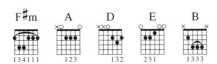

You hold the   fu - ture   in Your   hands. _

F♯m	A	D	E	B
134111	123	132	231	1333

Intro   ‖: F♯m | |A | :‖ *Play 4 times*

                           F♯m
Verse 1   You hold the future in Your hands.

                              A
               You know my dreams and You have a plan.

                         D   **A**   **F♯m**
               And as You light my way   I'll follow You.

                         D   **A**
Pre-Chorus 1   My eyes on all of the a - bove.

                   F♯m
               My soul se - cure in all You've done.

                            D   **A**   **E**
               My mind's made up and You are the only One for me.

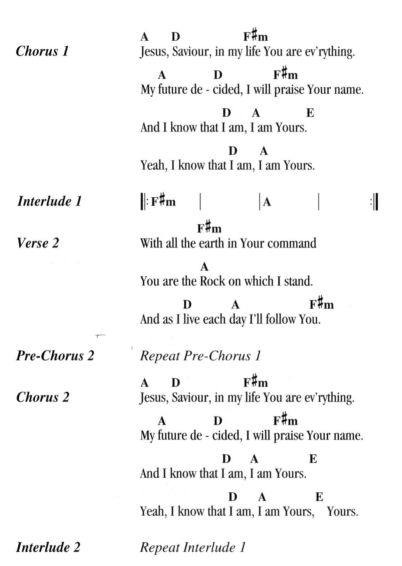

Chorus 1

A   D   F#m
Jesus, Saviour, in my life You are ev'rything.

A   D   F#m
My future de - cided, I will praise Your name.

D   A   E
And I know that I am, I am Yours.

D   A
Yeah, I know that I am, I am Yours.

Interlude 1

‖: F#m | |A | :‖

Verse 2

F#m
With all the earth in Your command

A
You are the Rock on which I stand.

D   A   F#m
And as I live each day I'll follow You.

Pre-Chorus 2

Repeat Pre-Chorus 1

Chorus 2

A   D   F#m
Jesus, Saviour, in my life You are ev'rything.

A   D   F#m
My future de - cided, I will praise Your name.

D   A   E
And I know that I am, I am Yours.

D   A   E
Yeah, I know that I am, I am Yours,   Yours.

Interlude 2

Repeat Interlude 1

Bridge

F♯m   **A**
Unafraid, unashamed, Lord, we know who we are.

(We are Your people and we won't be silent.)

F♯m   **A**
Unified, hear us cry at the top of our lungs.

(You are our God and we will not be shaken.)

F♯m   **A**
Unafraid, unashamed, Lord, we know who we are.

(We are Your people and we won't be silent.)

F♯m   **B**
Unified, hear us cry at the top of our lungs.

(You are our God and we will not be shaken.)

Chorus 3

    A   **D**   **F♯m**
‖: Jesus, Saviour, in my life You are ev'rything.

    A   **D**   **F♯m**
My future de - cided, I will praise Your name.

               D   **A**   **E**
And I know that I am, I am Yours.

               D   **A**   **E**
Yeah, I know that I am, I am Yours.   :‖

               D   **A**   **E**
‖: Yeah, I know that I am, I am Yours.   :‖

Jesus Generation

Words and Music by
Reuben Morgan

Melody:

Let the earth __ re - joice. __

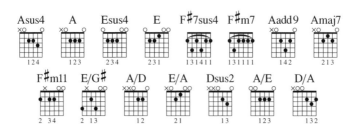

Intro

‖: Asus4   A |Asus4   A   :‖

Verse 1

        Asus4   A   Asus4 A
Let the earth ____ re - joice.

       Asus4 A   Asus4 A
See the ris - en   King

        Asus4   A   Asus4
On the clouds ____ of praise.

    A   Esus4 E
He's exalted for - ever.

Verse 2

        Asus4   A   Asus4 A
We will rise ____ to Him,

          Asus4   A   Asus4 A
The Son of Right - eous - ness.

       F#7sus4 F#m7
And the earth ____ will shake

F#7sus4 F#m7   Esus4 E
  With   the glory of Heav - en.

Chorus 1

        Aadd9   **Amaj7**
See the heav - ens open wide, and His glo - ry like a flood

        F#m11   **E/G#**   **A/D** **Esus4**
Fills the earth ___ with ___ salva - tion.

        Aadd9   **Amaj7**
See the na - tions take His hand, and in right - eousness they stand.

        F#m11 E/G#   **A/D** **Esus4**
This is Je - sus' ___ genera - tion.

Interlude 1   ‖: **Asus4**   **A** |**Asus4**   **A**   :‖

Verse 3   *Repeat Verse 2*

Chorus 2   *Repeat Chorus 1*

Interlude 2 |**E/A** **A** |**E/A** **A** |**A/D** **Dsus2** |**A/D** **Dsus2** |
                   |**A/E** **E** |**Esus4** **E** |**D/A** |**Esus4** |

Outro

      E/A **A E/A** **A A/D** **Dsus2 A/D Dsus2**
‖: Glo - ry, glo - ry, glo - ry.

      Esus4 **E Esus4 E**   **A/D**   **Esus4**
Em - manu - el, ____ God is with ___ us.   :‖ ***Play 4 times***

  E/A **A E/A** **A A/D** **Dsus2 A/D Dsus2**
Glo - ry, glo - ry, glo - ry.

     Esus4 **E Esus4 E**   **Dsus2**
Em - manu - el, ____ God is with ___ us.

Jesus I Long

Words and Music by
Marty Sampson

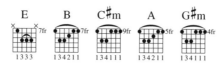

Intro

|E N.C. B N.C. |C#m N.C. |A N.C. E N.C. |B N.C. |

Verse 1

E N.C.   B N.C.   C#m N.C.
I need di - rec - tion in my life.

          A N.C.   E N.C.   B N.C.
Would You show   me Your way, 'cause I know it is ____ right.

E   B   C#m
And I need Your lovin' in my life.

          A   E   B
You're the only One whose love ____ is better than ____ life.

Chorus 1

A   E   B   C#m
Je - sus, I long to see Your face,

A   E   B
Je - sus, I long.

A   E   B   C#m
Je - sus, I long to see Your face,

A   E   B
Je - sus, I long.

Verse 2

E N.C.   B N.C.   C♯m N.C.
I need Your fa - vor in my life.

              A   E   B
Would You show me Your way, 'cause I know it is ___ right.

E   B   C♯m
And I need Your grace in my life.

              A   E   B
You're the only One whose love ___ is better than ___ life.

Chorus 2   *Repeat Chorus 1*

Interlude   ‖: G♯m A |E   :‖ *Play 3 times*
                |G♯m A |B |

Verse 3   *Repeat Verse 1*

Chorus 3

      A   E   B   C♯m
‖: Je - sus, I long to see Your face,

A   E   B
Je - sus, I long.

A   E   B   C♯m
Je - sus, I long to see Your face,

A   E   B
Je - sus, I long. :‖

|E   ‖

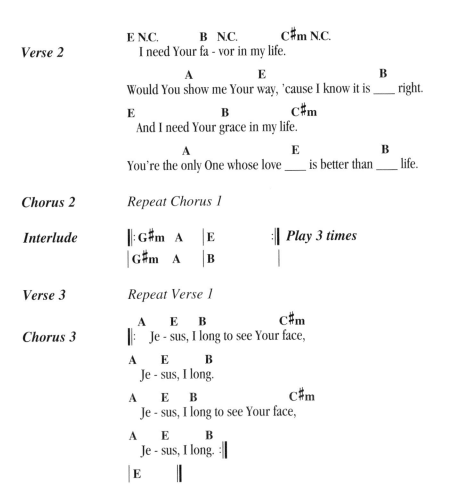

Jesus, Lover Of My Soul

Words and Music by John Ezzy,
Daniel Grul and Stephen McPherson

Wor - ship You,   my   Lord, _____

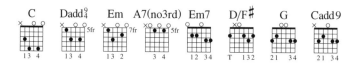

Intro

‖: C | Dadd$^9_4$ | Em | A7(no3rd) :‖

    C   Dadd$^9_4$ Em   C
‖: Worship You, my Lord, 'til the very end.

C   Dadd$^9_4$ Em A7(no3rd)
Worship You, my Lord,'til the very end.   :‖

| Em7 | D/F♯ | G | Cadd9 |
| Em7 | D/F♯ | Cadd9 | |

Verse 1

G   D/F♯
  Jesus, Lover of my soul.

Em7   D/F♯
  Jesus, I will never let You go.

G   D/F♯
  You've taken me from the miry clay,

Em7   Cadd9
  Set my feet upon the rock   and now I know.

Chorus 1

G   D/F#
I love You,   I need You.

Em7   Cadd9
Though my world may fall, I'll never let You go.

Em7   D/F#
My Savior,   my closest friend,

Cadd9
I will worship You until the very end.

Interlude

| Em7 | D/F# | G | Cadd9 | |
| Em7 | D/F# | Cadd9 | | |

Verse 2   *Repeat Verse 1*

Chorus 2   *Repeat Chorus 1*

Chorus 3   *Repeat Chorus 1*

Bridge

C Dadd$^{9}_{4}$ Em C
        My Lord, 'til the very end.

   C   Dadd$^{9}_{4}$ Em A7(no3rd)
‖: Worship You, my Lord, 'til the very end.

C   Dadd$^{9}_{4}$ Em C
Worship You, my Lord, 'til the very end. :‖ *Play 5 times*

Verse 3   *Repeat Verse 1*

Chorus 4   *Repeat Chorus 1*

King Of Majesty

Words and Music by
Marty Sampson

Melody:

You know that   I love You,

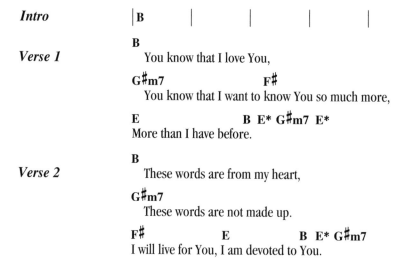

Intro |**B** | | | |

Verse 1
B
     You know that I love You,

G#m7   **F#**
     You know that I want to know You so much more,

E   **B E* G#m7 E***
More than I have before.

Verse 2
B
     These words are from my heart,

G#m7
     These words are not made up.

F#   **E**   **B E* G#m7**
I will live for You, I am devoted to You.

GUITAR CHORD SONGBOOK

Pre-Chorus 1

   E   F#   G#m7
King of Maj - esty, I have one ____ desire,

         F#   G#m7   E
Just to be ____ with You, ____ my Lord.

         F#   G#m7   E
Just to be ____ with You, ____ my Lord.

Chorus 1

  B E   F#   E   B G#m7 F#
Jesus, You are the Savior of my soul.

  E   B   G#m7 F#   E   B E F# E
And for - ever and ev - er I'll give my prais - es to You.

Verse 3   *Repeat Verse 1*

Verse 4   *Repeat Verse 2*

Pre-Chorus 2   *Repeat Pre-Chorus 1*

Chorus 2

  B E   F#   E   B G#m7 F#
‖: Jesus, You are the Savior of my soul.

  E   B   G#m7 F#   E   B E F# E
And for - ever and ev - er I'll give my prais - es to You.   :‖

Interlude | B   E | F# E | B G#m7 | F# E |

Chorus 3   *Repeat Chorus 2*

Chorus 4

  B E   F#   E   B G#m7 F#
‖: Jesus, You are the Savior of my soul.

  E   B   G#m7 F#   E   B E F# E
And for - ever and ev - er I'll give my prais - es to You.   :‖

| B   ‖

Kingdom Come

Words and Music by
Ben Fielding

Melody:

Your love   reach - es out __ to me,

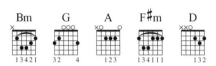

Bm G A F#m D

Intro ‖: **Bm** | | **G** | |
    | **A** | | **F#m G** | :‖

Verse 1
> **Bm**
> Your love reaches out to me.

> **G**   **A**
> Your grace has made a way to You,

>   **F#m G**
> Made a way to You.

> **Bm**
> Your Word lives inside of me.

> **G**   **A**
> Your truth is life to all who hear,

>   **G**
> Life to all who hear.

Pre-Chorus 1
>   **A**   **G**
> We live for You, ___ live Your truth.

Chorus 1
>   **D**   **G**
> May Your Kingdom come and Your will be done

>   **Bm**   **G**
> As we serve ___ Your heart, serve Your heart.

>   **D**   **G**
> Let sal - vation flow as Your people pray.

>   **Bm**   **G**
> Lord, we long ___ for more, long for more.

Interlude

```
|Bm        |          |G        |          |
|A         |          |F♯m    G |          |
```

Verse 2

Bm
In You death is overcome.

G   A
No power can stand against Your name,

       F♯m G
The power of Your name.

Bm
In faith we will rise to be

G   A
Your hands and feet to all the earth,

       G
Life to all the earth.

Pre-Chorus 2

Repeat Pre-Chorus 1

Chorus 2

Repeat Chorus 1

Bridge

```
|Bm        |          |G        |          |
|A         |          |G        |          |
```

Bm   G   A   G
Lord, we long for You, ___ to see Your truth ___ in all we do.

```
|Bm        |          |G        |          |
|A         |          |G        |          |
```

Pre-Chorus 3

      A   G
We live for You, ___ live Your truth.

      A   G
We long for You, ___ to see Your truth.

Chorus 3

Repeat Chorus 1

Chorus 4

Repeat Chorus 1

Outro

```
||:Bm      |          |G        |          |
|A         |          |G        |        :||
```

Lead Me To The Cross

Words and Music by
Brooke Fraser

Melody:

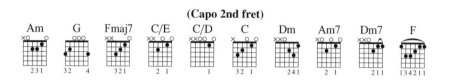

Sav-iour, I come, _ qui - et my _ soul. _

(Capo 2nd fret)

Am   G   Fmaj7   C/E   C/D   C   Dm   Am7   Dm7   F

Intro
| Am G | Fmaj7 C/E C/D | Am G | Fmaj7 | |

Verse 1
    Am   G   Fmaj7
Saviour, I come, ___ quiet my soul.

    C   G Am   G
Re-member ___ redemption's hill,

                  Fmaj7   C   G
Where Your blood was spilled for my ran - som.

Pre-Chorus 1
    Dm   G
Ev'rything I once held dear,

          Am   G   Fmaj7
I count ___ it all as loss.

Chorus 1
            Fmaj7   C   G
Lead me to the cross where Your love poured out.

           Fmaj7   C   G
Bring me to my knees, Lord, I lay me down.

Am7   Fmaj7   C   G
Rid me of my - self, I be - long to You.

         Dm7 Fmaj7 G   Am G Fmaj7 C
Oh, lead me, ___ lead me to the cross.

| Am G | Fmaj7 C | |

Verse 2

Am   G   Fmaj7   C G
You were as I, ___ tempted and tried, ___ hu - man.

Am   G
The Word became flesh,

                   Fmaj7   C G
Bore my sin in death ___ now You're ris - en.

Pre-Chorus 2   *Repeat Pre-Chorus 1*

Chorus 2

N.C.   Fmaj7   C   G
Lead me to the cross where Your love poured out.

               Fmaj7   C   G
Bring me to my knees, Lord, I lay me down.

Am7   Fmaj7   C   G
Rid me of my - self, I be - long to You.

              Dm7 Fmaj7 G   Am F
Oh, lead me, ___ lead me to the cross.

Bridge

           C Fmaj7 G
‖: To Your heart.   :‖

              C Fmaj7 G
‖: Lead me to Your heart.   :‖

Chorus 3

              Fmaj7   C   G
Lead me to the cross where Your love poured out.

               Fmaj7   C   G
Bring me to my knees, Lord, I lay me down.

Am   Amaj7   C   G
Rid me of my - self, I be - long to You.

              Dm7   F
Oh, lead me, ___ lead ___ me,

G   Fmaj7   C   G
Lead me to the cross where Your love poured out.

               Fmaj7   C   G
Bring me to my knees, Lord, I lay me down.

Am   Fmaj7   C   G
Rid me of my - self, I be - long to You.

              Dm7 F   G   N.C.
Oh, lead me, ___ lead me to the cross.

Look To You

Words and Music by
Marty Sampson

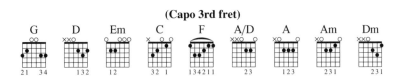

(Capo 3rd fret)

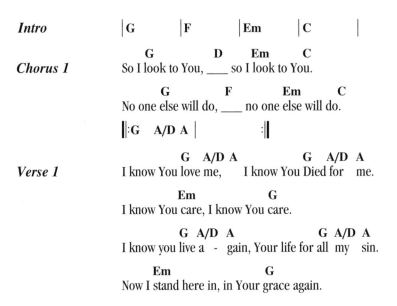

Intro |G |F |Em |C |

Chorus 1
        G   **D**   **Em**   **C**
So I look to You, ___ so I look to You.

           G   **F**   **Em**   **C**
No one else will do, ___ no one else will do.

||: **G** **A/D A** | :||

Verse 1
          G A/D A   **G A/D A**
I know You love me, I know You Died for me.

           Em   **G**
I know You care, I know You care.

          G A/D A   **G A/D A**
I know you live a - gain, Your life for all my sin.

           Em   **G**
Now I stand here in, in Your grace again.

Pre-Chorus 1

        C   D
When I look into the sky ___ above,

C   Am
Wonder how my life ___ has changed,

C   Em   D
Wonder how Your love, ___ it came to me.

        C   D
When I look into the sky ___ above,

C   Am
All my fears so far ___ away,

       C   Em   D
And all I feel is heav - en calling me.

Chorus 2   *Repeat Chorus 1*

Verse 2   *Repeat Verse 1*

Pre-Chorus 2   *Repeat Pre-Chorus 1*

Chorus 3

        G   D   Em   C
‖: So I look to You, ___ so I look to You.

        G   F   Em   C
No one else will do, ___ no one else will do. :‖

Interlude

‖:G | |Dm | |
|Am | |C | :‖

Pre-Chorus 3   *Repeat Pre-Chorus 1*

Chorus 4

        G   D   Em   C
‖: So I look to You, ___ so I look to You.

        G   F   Em   C
No one else will do, ___ no one else will do. :‖ *Play 6 times*

More

Words and Music by
Reuben Morgan

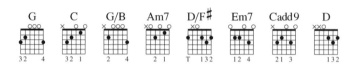

G · C · G/B · Am7 · D/F♯ · Em7 · Cadd9 · D

32 4	32 1	2 4	2 1	T 132	12 4	21 3	132

Intro ‖: G | C | G | C :‖

Verse 1
G   C G   C
I will wait,   reach out my hands ___ before You.

G   C G   C G/B Am7   G   D/F♯
My keeper,   I will come run - ning in - to Your ___ arms.

   G   D/F♯ Em7   Am7   G   D/F♯
It's You I long ___ for ___ with all my ___ heart.

Chorus 1
Cadd9   D   Em7
I want to know ___ You,

Cadd9   D   Em7
You are all ___ I want.

Cadd9   D   Em7 Cadd9 D Em7
I want to know ___ You   more.

| Cadd9 | D Em7 | Cadd9 | D | |

Verse 2 *Repeat Verse 1*

GUITAR CHORD SONGBOOK

Chorus 2	**Cadd9** **D** **Em7** ‖: I want to know ___ You,

Cadd9   **D**   **Em7**
You are all ___ I want.

Cadd9   **D**   **Em7 Cadd9 D Em7**
I want to know ___ You   more.   :‖

Interlude   ‖: **Cadd9** │**D**   **Em7** :‖ *Play 12 times*

Chorus 3
Cadd9   **D**   **Em7**
‖: I want to know ___ You,

Cadd9   **D**   **Em7**
You are all ___ I want.

Cadd9   **D**   **Em7 Cadd9 D Em7**
I want to know ___ You   more.   :‖

│**Cmaj9**   ‖

More Than Life

Words and Music by
Reuben Morgan

Melody:

Stand by ev - 'ry - thing _ You said. _

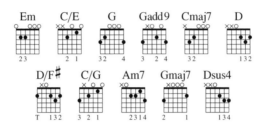

| Em | C/E | G | Gadd9 | Cmaj7 | D |
| D/F♯ | C/G | Am7 | Gmaj7 | Dsus4 | |

Intro　　　‖: Em C/E | G Gadd9 :‖ *Play 4 times*

Verse 1

Em　　　　　C/E　　　　G Gadd9
Stand by ev - 'rything You said.

Em　　　　　　　C/E　　　G　Gadd9
Stand by the prom - ises we made.

Em　　　　C/E　　　　G　Gadd9
Let go of ev - 'rything I've done.

Em　　　　C/E　　　　G　Gadd9
I'll run into ____ Your open arms.

Cmaj7　　　　　　D
And all I know ____ is that...

Chorus 1

Em D/F♯ G C/G　　　　Em C/E G Gadd9
I　　love　You more than life.

Em D/F♯ G C/G　　　　Em C/E G Gadd9
I　　love　You more than life.

Verse 2

Em   C/E   G Gadd9
Fall back on ev - 'rything You've done.

Em   C/E G Gadd9
Fall back on everlasting arms.

Em   C/E   G Gadd9
When all the world is swept a-way,

Em   C/E   G Gadd9
You are all the things I need.

Cmaj7   D
You're the air I breathe.

Chorus 2

 Em D/F♯ G C/G   Em C/E G Gadd9
‖: I love You more than life.

Em D/F♯ G C/G   Em C/E G Gadd9
I love You more than life.   :‖

Interlude ‖: Am7 |Gmaj7 |Em |Dsus4 D :‖ *Play 4 times*

Bridge

Cmaj7   D   Em   Cmaj7
And how can it be ___ You were the One ___ on the cross,

Am7   D   Em D/F♯ G
Lifted for all ___ our shame?

Cmaj7   D   Em   Cmaj7
And how can it be ___ the scars in Your hands ___ are for me?

Am7   D   G D
You are the King ___ of all.

Chorus 3

 Em D/F♯ G C/G   Em C/E G Gadd9
‖: I love You more than life.

Em D/F♯ G C/G   Em C/E G Gadd9
I love You more than life.   :‖

Em D/F♯ G C/G   Em C/E G
I love You more than life.

Most High

Words and Music by
Reuben Morgan

Melody:

I want to see Your __ face, __

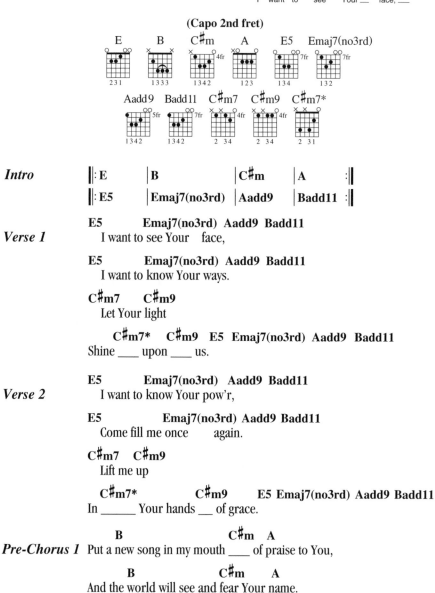

(Capo 2nd fret)

E   B   C#m   A   E5   Emaj7(no3rd)

Aadd9   Badd11   C#m7   C#m9   C#m7*

Intro

‖: E | B | C#m | A :‖

‖: E5 | Emaj7(no3rd) | Aadd9 | Badd11 :‖

Verse 1

E5 Emaj7(no3rd) Aadd9 Badd11
I want to see Your face,

E5 Emaj7(no3rd) Aadd9 Badd11
I want to know Your ways.

C#m7 C#m9
Let Your light

 C#m7* C#m9 E5 Emaj7(no3rd) Aadd9 Badd11
Shine ___ upon ___ us.

Verse 2

E5 Emaj7(no3rd) Aadd9 Badd11
I want to know Your pow'r,

E5 Emaj7(no3rd) Aadd9 Badd11
Come fill me once again.

C#m7 C#m9
Lift me up

C#m7* C#m9 E5 Emaj7(no3rd) Aadd9 Badd11
In _____ Your hands __ of grace.

Pre-Chorus 1

  B   C#m   A
Put a new song in my mouth ___ of praise to You,

  B   C#m A
And the world will see and fear Your name.

	E B C#m A
Chorus 1	Worthy, worthy ___ is the Lord.

                 E   B   C#m   A
Worthy,   worthy ___ is the Lord.

              E   B   C#m   A
Worthy, ____ worthy ___ is the Lord

                E   B C#m A
Most ___ high.

Interlude |E5 |Emaj7(no3rd) |Aadd9 |Gadd11 |

Verse 3 *Repeat Verse 2*

             B   C#m   A
Pre-Chorus 2 ‖: Put a new song in my mouth ___ of praise to You,

             B   C#m   A
And the world will see and fear Your name.   :‖

             E   B   C#m   A
Chorus 2 ‖: Worthy,   worthy ___ is the Lord.

              E   B   C#m   A
Worthy,   worthy ___ is the Lord.

              E   B   C#m   A
Worthy,   worthy ___ is the Lord

              E   B C#m B
Most ___ high.   :‖

Interlude 2 ‖: E |B |C#m |A :‖ *Play 4 times*

Pre-Chorus 3 *Repeat Pre-Chorus 2*

Chorus 3 *Repeat Chorus 2*

Outro ‖: E |B |C#m |A :‖
       |E ‖

My Best Friend

Words and Music by
Joel Houston and Marty Sampson

Melody:

Have you heard of the One called Sav - iour?

C   G   F♯   Am7   Fadd9

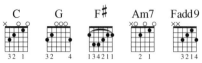

Intro   ‖:C   G |F   G |C   G |F   G :‖

Verse 1
C N.C.   G   F
Have you heard of the One called Sav - iour?

N.C.   G   C
Have you heard of His perfect love?

N.C.   G   F
Have you heard of the One in heav - en?

N.C.
Have you heard how He gave His Son?

Am7   G   F
Well, I have found this love,   and I believe in the Son.

Show me Your way.

Interlude 1 |C   G |F   G |C   G |F   G |

Verse 2
C N.C.   G   F
I believe in the One called Sav - iour.

N.C.   G   C
I believe He's the Risen One.

N.C.   G   F
I believe that I'll live forev - er.

N.C.
I believe that the King will come.

Am7   G   F
'Cause I have found this love,   and I believe in the Son.

Show me Your way.

Chorus 1

         C   G   Am7

‖: Jesus, You are my best friend, ___ and You will always be,

                 F

And nothing will ever change that. :‖

Interlude 2   *Repeat Interlude 1*

Verse 3   *Repeat Verse 2*

Chorus 2

        C   G   Am7

‖: Jesus, You are my best friend, and You will always be,

                 F

And nothing will ever change that.

C   G   Am7

Jesus, You are my best friend, and You will always be,

                 F

And nothing will ever change that. :‖

Bridge

  | C | Am7 | G | Fadd9 |

     C   Am7   G

‖:   Nothing will ev - er change that.

             Fadd9

Nothing will ev - er change that.   :‖ *Play 4 times*

Chorus 3   *Repeat Chorus 2*

Outro

     C   Am7

‖:   No, nothing will ev - er change that.

G   F

   No, nothing will ev - er change that. :‖

My God

Words and Music by
Marty Sampson

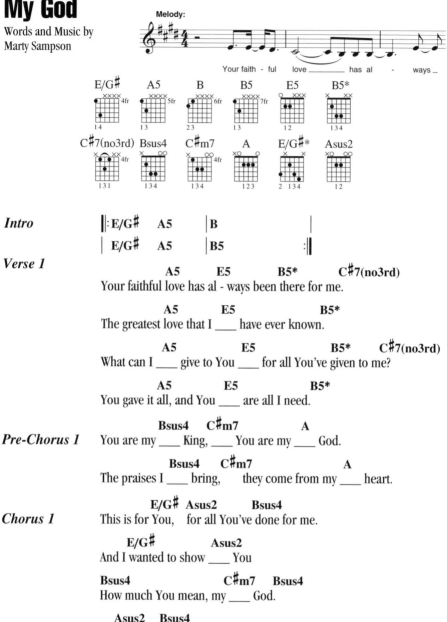

Melody:

Your faith - ful love _____ has al - ways _

Intro

‖: E/G♯　A5　|B　　　|
| E/G♯　A5　|B5　　　:‖

Verse 1

　　　　　A5　　E5　　　B5*　　　C♯7(no3rd)
Your faithful love has al - ways been there for me.

　　　　　A5　　E5　　　　　B5*
The greatest love that I ____ have ever known.

　　　　　A5　　　　E5　　　　　B5*　　C♯7(no3rd)
What can I ____ give to You ____ for all You've given to me?

　　　　　A5　　　E5　　　　B5*
You gave it all, and You ____ are all I need.

Pre-Chorus 1

　　　　　Bsus4　C♯m7　　　　　A
You are my ____ King, ____ You are my ____ God.

　　　　　Bsus4　　C♯m7　　　　　　A
The praises I ____ bring, 　 they come from my ____ heart.

Chorus 1

　　　　　E/G♯　Asus2　　　Bsus4
This is for You, 　 for all You've done for me.

　　E/G♯　　　　　Asus2
And I wanted to show ____ You

Bsus4　　　　　　　　C♯m7　Bsus4
How much You mean, my ____ God.

　　　Asus2　Bsus4
My ____ God.

| Verse 2 | Repeat Verse 1 |

Verse 2 Repeat Verse 1

Pre-Chorus 2 Repeat Pre-Chorus 1

Chorus 2

           E/G♯ Asus2   **Bsus4**
‖: This is for You,   for all You've done for me.

      E/G♯   **Asus2**
And I wanted to show ____ You

Bsus4   **C♯m7**   **Bsus4**
How much You mean, my ____ God.

      Asus2   **Bsus4**
My ____ God.   :‖

Interlude

‖: **C♯m7** | **Bsus4** | **A** | :‖

Bridge

            E/G♯ Asus2 B
‖: This is for You.   :‖ *Play 8 times*

Chorus 3 Repeat Chorus 1

Chorus 4

           E/G♯ Asus2   **Bsus4**
This is for You,   for all You've done for me.

      E/G♯   **Asus2**
And I wanted to show ____ You

Bsus4   **C♯m7**   **Bsus4**
How much You mean, my ____ God.

      Asus2
My ____ God.

Need You Here

Words and Music by
Reuben Morgan

Melody:

I _____ need _You here, _____

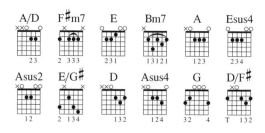

A/D   F#m7   E   Bm7   A   Esus4

Asus2   E/G#   D   Asus4   G   D/F#

Intro

| A/D | | |

‖: A/D   F#m7 E | A/D   F#m7 E :‖ *Play 3 times*

Verse 1

A/D F#m7   E A/D F#m7 E
I   need You here,

A/D F#m7   E   A/D F#m7 E
I   need You here.

A/D F#m7 E   A/D F#m7 E
You're like the rain that falls,

A/D   F#m7   E   A/D   F#m7 E A/D F#m7 E
Fall on this heart and make me ___ new.

Verse 2

A/D F#m7 E A/D F#m7 E
I   look to You,

A/D F#m7 E A/D F#m7 E
I   look to You.

A/D F#m7 E   A/D F#m7 E
You're King a - bove the earth,

    A/D   F#m7 E   Bm7   A
And You have put heaven in my ___ heart.

Pre-Chorus 1

Esus4 E   Bm7   A   Esus4 E
I only wanna be ___ where ___ You are.

Chorus 1

Asus2 E/G#   D   Esus4
Holy,   holy is the Lord, ___ King of Glory.

    Asus4 A E/G#   Bm7 E
For - ev - er Saviour of the world.

Interlude 1

| A/D   F#m7 E | A/D   F#m7 E |

Verse 3   *Repeat Verse 2*

Pre-Chorus 2   *Repeat Pre-Chorus 1*

Chorus 2

   Asus2 E/G#   D   Esus4
‖: Holy,   holy is the Lord, ___ King of Glory.

    Asus4 A E/G#   Bm7 E
For - ev - er Saviour of the world.   :‖

Saviour of the world.

Interlude 2

G	D/F#	A	Esus4 E
G	D/F#	Esus4	E
A/D F#m7 E	A/D F#m7 E	A/D F#m7 E	A/D F#m7 E

Verse 4

A/D   F#m7   E   A/D F#m7 E
Though mountains may be moved,

   A/D   F#m7 E   A/D   F#m7 E
And fall in - to the raging ___ seas,

A/D F#m7 E   A/D F#m7 E
You'll never   let me fall.

A/D   F#m7 E   Bm7   A
You hold me in Your nail scarred ___ hands.

Pre-Chorus 3

Esus4 E   Bm7   A   E
        I only wanna be ___ where ___ You are.

          Bm7   A   E
I only wanna be ___ where ___ You are.

          Bm7   A   E
I only wanna be ___ where ___ You are.

Chorus 3   *Repeat Chorus 1*

Chorus 4

Asus2 E/G♯   D   Esus4
Holy,   holy is the Lord, ___ King of Glory.

    Asus4 A E/G♯   G
For - ev - er Saviour of the world.

                D/F♯   Esus4 E
Saviour of the world. ___ Saviour of the world.

          G   D/F♯ E
Saviour of the world.

Open Up The Heavens

Words and Music by
Joel Houston

Melody:

O - pen up __ the heav - ens,

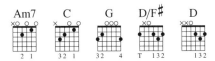

Am7   C   G   D/F#   D

Intro

‖: Am7 |C |G |D/F# :‖

Chorus

   Am7   C   G   D/F#
‖: Open up the heav - ens, and let Your glory fall.

Am7   C   G   D/F#
Open up our hearts ___ that we would know ___ You.

Am7   C   G   D/F#
Open up the heav - ens, and let Your glory fall.

Am7   C G   D/F#
Open up our hearts, ___ open up our hearts. :‖

Outro

|Am7 |C |G |D/F# ‖

Now That You're Near

Words and Music by
Marty Sampson

Melody:

I stand be-fore You, Lord, __

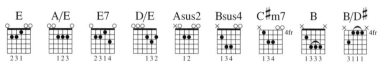

E   A/E   E7   D/E   Asus2   Bsus4   C#m7   B   B/D#

| | | | | | | | | |
231   123   2314   132   12   134   134   1333   3111

Intro   ‖: E |A/E |E7 |D/E   :‖ *Play 3 times*

Verse 1
    E   Asus2   C#m7
I stand before You, Lord, ____ and give You all my praise.

                          Asus2   Bsus4
Your love is all that I need. ____ Jesus, ____ You're all I need.

Verse 2
    E   Asus2   C#m7
My life belongs to You, ____ You gave Your life for me.

                          Asus2   Bsus4
Your grace is all that I need. ____ Jesus, ____ You're all I need.

Pre-Chorus 1
C#m7   Asus2   E   B
Hold me in Your arms,   never let me go.

C#m7   Asus2   E   B
I want to spend e - ternity with You.

Chorus 1
         E   B   C#m7
And now that You're near, ev'rything is diff'rent,

              Asus2
Ev'rything's so diff'rent, Lord.

         E   B   C#m7
And I know I'm not the same, ____ my life You've changed.

                    Asus2   E A/E E7 D/E
And I wanna be with You, ____ I wanna be with You.

Verse 3   *Repeat Verse 1*

Verse 4   *Repeat Verse 2*

Pre-Chorus 2   *Repeat Pre-Chorus 1*

Chorus 2

      E   B   C#m7
And now that You're near, ev'rything is diff'rent,

          Asus
Ev'rything's so diff'rent, Lord.

      E   B   C#m7
And I know I'm not the same, ___ my life You've changed.

             Asus2   E
And I wanna be with You, ___ I wanna be with You.

Chorus 3

        B   C#m7
Now that You're near, ev'rything is diff'rent,

          Asus2
Ev'rything's so diff'rent, Lord.

      E   B   C#m7
And I know I'm not the same, ___ my life You've changed.

             Asus2   C#m7
And I wanna be with You, ___ I wanna be with You.

Bridge

        Asus2   E B
And I will sing ___ for You, always,

C#m7   Bsus4   Asus2
 'Cause in Your pres - ence, Lord, is where ___ I want to stay.

Interlude   ‖: C#m7 Asus2 │E   Bsus4 :‖

Pre-Chorus 3   *Repeat Pre-Chorus 1*

Chorus 4   *Repeat Chorus 2*

Chorus 5

        B/D#   C#m7
Now You're near, ev'rything is diff'rent,

          Asus2
Ev'rything's so diff'rent, Lord.

      E   B   C#m7
And I know I'm not the same, ___ my life You've changed.

             Asus2   E
And I wanna be with You, ___ I wanna be with You.

Outro   ‖: E   │A/E   │E7   │D/E   :‖
          │E   ‖

On The Lord's Day

Words and Music by
Reuben Morgan

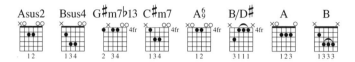

Make a way   for the __ love __ of God. __

Asus2 Bsus4 G#m7b13 C#m7 A⁶₉ B/D# A B

Intro

‖: Asus2 Bsus4 | G#m7b13 C#m7 :‖ *Play 4 times*

Verse 1

Asus2 Bsus4 G#m7b13 C#m7
Make a way   for the   love of God.

Asus2 Bsus4   G#m7b13 C#m7   Asus4 A⁶₉
Let   the world know that He is near.

Verse 2

Asus2 Bsus4   G#m7b13   C#m7
Val - leys rise, mountains will be moved

Asus2 Bsus4   G#m7b13 C#m7 Asus2
As   our praise rises up   to You.

Bsus4 Asus2   B/D#
I will pray.   I will pray.

Chorus 1

A   Bsus4   C#m7 G#m7b13
Let Your Kingdom come,

A   Bsus4   A Bsus4
Pray Your will be done.

A   Bsus4   C#m7 G#m7b13
Nations will see Your fame

A   Bsus4   Asus2 Bsus4 G#m7b13 C#m7
On the Lord's day.

| Asus2 Bsus4 | G#m7b13 C#m7 |

Verse 3	*Repeat Verse 1*
Verse 4	*Repeat Verse 2*

Chorus 2

A   Bsus4   C#m7 G#m7♭13
Let Your Kingdom come,

A   Bsus4   A Bsus4
Pray Your will be done.

A   Bsus4   C#m7 G#m7♭13
Nations will see Your fame

A   Bsus4   G#m7♭13 A Bsus4
On the Lord's day.

Chorus 3

A   Bsus4   C#m7 G#m7♭13
Let Your Kingdom come,

A   Bsus4   A Bsus4
Pray Your will be done.

A   Bsus4   C#m7 G#m7♭13
Nations will see Your fame

A   Bsus4   Asus2 A§
On the Lord's day.

Bridge

‖: Asus2 |A§   :‖ *Play 3 times*

    Asus2   A§
‖: I will pray. :‖ *Play 3 times*

Asus2   B
I will pray.

Chorus 4	*Repeat Chorus 2*
Chorus 5	*Repeat Chorus 1*

Outro

|Asus2 Bsus4 |G#m7♭13 C#m7 |Asus2 Bsus4 |Asus2 ‖

One Way

Words and Music by Joel Houston
and Jonathon Douglass

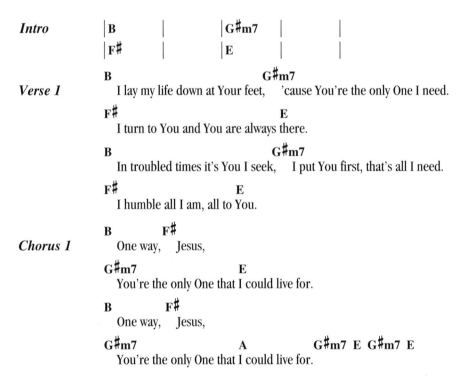

Intro |B | |G#m7 | |
         |F# | |E | |

Verse 1

    B   G#m7
I lay my life down at Your feet,   'cause You're the only One I need.

    F#   E
I turn to You and You are always there.

    B   G#m7
In troubled times it's You I seek,   I put You first, that's all I need.

    F#   E
I humble all I am, all to You.

Chorus 1

    B   F#
One way,   Jesus,

    G#m7   E
You're the only One that I could live for.

    B   F#
One way,   Jesus,

    G#m7   A   G#m7 E G#m7 E
You're the only One that I could live for.

© 2003 Joel Houston, Jonathan Douglass and Hillsong Publishing
(admin. in the United States and Canada by Integrity's Hosanna! Music/ASCAP)
c/o Integrity Media, Inc., 1000 Cody Road, Mobile, AL 36695
All Rights Reserved   International Copyright Secured   Used by Permission

Verse 2

B   G♯m7
You are always, always there,   ev'ry how and ev'rywhere.

F♯   E
Your grace abounds so deeply within me.

B   G♯m7
You will never, ever change,   yesterday, today the same.

F♯   E
Forever 'til forever meets no end.

Chorus 2

     B   F♯
‖:   One way,   Jesus,

G♯m7   E
You're the only One that I could live for.

B   F♯
One way,   Jesus,

G♯m7   A
You're the only One that I could live for. :‖

Bridge

     B   F♯
‖: You are the way, the truth ___ and the life.

      G♯m7   E   G♯m7
We live ___ by faith and not ___ by sight for You.

      F♯   E
We're liv - ing all for You. :‖ ***Play 4 times***

Chorus 3

     B   F♯
‖:   One way,   Jesus,

G♯m7   E
You're the only One that I could live for.

B   F♯
One way,   Jesus,

G♯m7   A
You're the only One that I could live for. :‖

  |B   ‖

Perfect King

Words and Music by
Damian Bassett

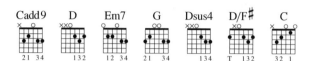

Cadd9   D   Em7   G   Dsus4   D/F#   C

Intro

| Cadd9 | D | Em7 | G | |
| Cadd9 | D | Em7 | D | |

Verse 1

  G   Dsus4
    I've come to love on You.

  Em7   D/F# G
    I've come to pledge my life to You.

              Dsus4   Em7   Dsus4 D
    I've come to sit at Your feet and sing sweet songs to You.

| Cadd9 | | |

Verse 2

  G   Dsus4
    I've come to give my life

  Em7   D/F# G
    To the greatest Love of   all.

              Dsus4   Em7
    I've come to lift my hands to You,

           D   Em7
    The desi - re of my heart,

           D   C D
    The Lov - er of my soul.

Chorus 1

Cadd9   Dsus4   Em7
And I ___ will wor - ship You with all ___ my heart,

D/F♯   G
For You are worthy.

Cadd9 Dsus4   Em7   D   Cadd9 D
And I will bow ___ to You, my per - fect King,   Jesus.

Verse 3   *Repeat Verse 2*

Chorus 2

Cadd9   Dsus4   Em7
‖: And I ___ will wor - ship You with all ___ my heart,

D/F♯   G
For You are worthy.

Cadd9 Dsus4   Em7   D
And I will bow ___ to You, my per - fect King,   Jesus. :‖

Interlude   *Repeat Intro*

Bridge

Cadd9   D   Em7 G
‖: I love You, ___ Jesus.

Cadd9   D   Em7 D
I love You, ___ Jesus.   :‖ *Play 3 times*

Chorus 3

Cadd9   Dsus4   Em7
‖: And I ___ will wor - ship You with all ___ my heart,

D/F♯   G
For You are worthy.

Cadd9 Dsus4   Em7   D   C
And I will bow ___ to You, my per - fect King,   Jesus. :‖

Outro

| Dsus4 | Em7 | G | Cadd9 | |
| Dsus4 | Em7 | Dsus4 | Cadd9 | ‖ |

Point Of Difference

Words and Music by
Joel Houston

Melody:

The tide is turn - ing,

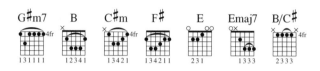

G#m7   B   C#m   F#   E   Emaj7   B/C#

Intro |G#m7 |B   C#m |G#m7 |B   C#m |

Verse 1
> G#m7   B
>   The tide is turning, this is re - demption's hour.
>
>   C#m   G#m7
> In the midst ____ of a world lost for love
>
>   F#   E
> You are all we have ____ now.
>
> G#m7   B
>   The lost returning, salvation is all around.
>
>   C#m   G#m7
> In the midst ____ of a world broken down
>
>   F#   E
> You are all we have ____ now.
>
>   G#m7 E
> For You are God and this hope   is ours.
>
>
> So Father…

Chorus 1
> B   F#
> Open the skies, flood the earth with Your light.
>
>   G#m7   E
> This is love to break a world in - different.

Interlude ||: G#m7 | |B | C#m :||

Verse 2

G#m7   B
　Our hearts are burning a fire that won't burn out.

　　　　　C#m   G#m7
In the midst ___ of a world that's grown cold

　　　　F#   E
You are all we have ___ now.

G#m7   B
　The earth resounding the anthem of Your renown.

　　　C#m   G#m7   F#
As we lift up our eyes and look ___ to Your glory.

Pre-Chorus 1

Emaj7   G#m7
Call us out, let the world see

Emaj7   G#m7   B
You are God, and this hope is ___ ours.

　　Emaj7   G#m7   Emaj7
So call us out, let the world see You are God,

As we sing…

Chorus 2

B   F#
Open the skies, flood the earth with Your light.

　　G#m7   E
This is love to break a world in - different.

　　B   F#
As we lift up our eyes, fill our hearts with Your fire.

　G#m7   E
In a world the same, we'll be the dif - ferent, the difference.

Emaj7   G#m7
Call us out, let the world see

Emaj7   B   C#m
You are God, and this hope is ___ ours.

| G#m7 | | E | |

                                 B
Bridge   Our eyes are open, every chain now broken.

                                 B/C# G#m7   **E**
                            We're in this ___ world, but we are different.

                                     B
                            Let Your love become us as we live to make You famous.

                                 B/C# G#m7   **E**
                            We're in this ___ world, but we are different.

                                 Emaj7   **G#m7**
Pre-Chorus 2   So call us out, let the world see

                            Emaj7
                            You are God, as we sing…

                            B   **F#**
Chorus 3   Open the skies, flood the earth with Your light.

                                 G#m7   **E**
                            This is love to break a world in - different.

                                     B   **F#**
                            As we lift up our eyes fill our hearts with Your fire.

                                 G#m7   **E**
                            In a world the same, we'll be the dif - ferent, the difference.

                            Emaj7   **G#m7**
                            Call us out, let the world see

                            Emaj7   **G#m7**
                            You are God, one and only.

                            Emaj7   **G#m7 E**
                            In this world You are all we have now.

Salvation Is Here

Words and Music by Joel Houston

Melody:

God a - bove with the world in ___ mo - tion.

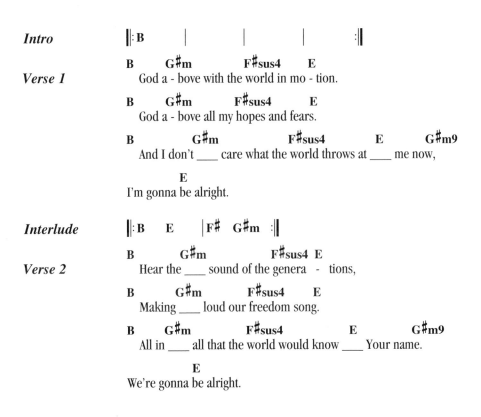

Intro   ‖: B | | | :‖

Verse 1

B   G#m   F#sus4   E
God a - bove with the world in mo - tion.

B   G#m   F#sus4   E
God a - bove all my hopes and fears.

B   G#m   F#sus4   E   G#m9
And I don't ___ care what the world throws at ___ me now,

                E
I'm gonna be alright.

Interlude   ‖: B   E |F#   G#m :‖

Verse 2

B   G#m   F#sus4 E
Hear the ___ sound of the genera - tions,

B   G#m   F#sus4   E
Making ___ loud our freedom song.

B   G#m   F#sus4   E   G#m9
All in ___ all that the world would know ___ Your name.

                E
We're gonna be alright.

Chorus 1	**B** **E**
	'Cause I know my God ____ saved the day.
	
	      F♯ **G♯m**
	And I know ____ His word ____ never fails.
	
	      B **E** **C♯m**
	And I know ____ my God ____ made a way for me.
	
	E **B**
	   Salvation is ____ here.

Verse 3	*Repeat Verse 1*

Chorus 2	**B** **E**
	'Cause I know my God ____ saved the day.
	
	      F♯ **G♯m**
	And I know ____ His Word ____ never fails.
	
	      B **E** **C♯m**
	And I know ____ my God ____ made a way for me.
	
	      E
	It's gonna be alright.

Chorus 3	**B** **E**
	'Cause I know my God ____ saved the day.
	
	      F♯ **G♯m**
	And I know ____ His Word ____ never fails.
	
	      B **E** **C♯m**
	And I know ____ my God ____ made a way for me.
	
	E
	   Salvation is here.

Bridge |G#m |B |E |C#m |
               |G#m |B |E |C#m |

                   G#m   B   E   C#m
Salvation is ___ here,   salvation is here and He lives in me.

                   G#m   B   E   C#m
Salvation is ___ here,   salvation that died just to set me free.

                   G#m   B   E   C#m
Salvation is ___ here.   Salvation is here and He lives in me.

                   G#m   B   E   C#m
Salvation is ___ here,   'cause You are alive ___ and You live in me.

                     B   E   F#   G#m
Salvation is ___ here.   Salvation is here and He lives in me.

                     B   E   F#   G#m
Salvation is ___ here,   'cause You are alive ___ and You live in me.

Chorus 4   *Repeat Chorus 2*

                 B   E
Chorus 5   'Cause I know my God ___ saved the day.

                 F#   G#m
And I know ___ His Word ___ never fails.

                 B   E   C#m
And I know ___ my God ___ made a way for me.

E   B
  Salvation is ___ here.

E   F#   G#m
  Salvation is here and He lives in me.

             B   E   F#   G#m
Salvation is ___ here,   'cause You are alive ___ and You live in me.

             B
Salvation is ___ here.

Prayer To The King

Words and Music by
Marty Sampson

Melody:

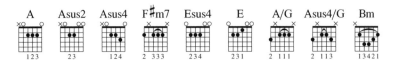

We seek _ the Son of __ God. ___

A   Asus2   Asus4   F#m7   Esus4   E   A/G   Asus4/G   Bm

Intro   ‖: A Asus2 | Asus4 A | | :‖ *Play 4 times*

Verse 1
    A   Asus2 Asus4 A
    We seek the Son of God.

                       Asus2 Asus4 A
    We seek the Risen Lord.

    F#m7
    We seek the King of Kings,

                 A   Asus2 Asus4 A
    The Saviour of the world.

Verse 2
    A   Asus2 Asus4 A
    We give our lives to You.

                     Asus2 Asus4 A
    We choose to follow You.

    F#m7   Esus4 E
    We believe in You. We worship You.

Chorus 1

A   Asus4 A   A/G   Asus4/G
We seek Your face and _____ humble our - selves here.

A/G F#m7   Esus4 Bm
The fire of God consuming the hearts of man.

A   Asus4 A   A/G   Asus4/G
Nations will bow to You. _____ Kingdoms will shake before You.

A/G   F#m7 Esus4   Bm
We pray for re - vival,   we pray for re - vival.

| A Asus2 | Asus4 A | | | |

Verse 3

A   Asus2 Asus4 A
We seek the Son of God.

Asus2 Asus4 A
We seek the Risen Lord.

F#m7
We seek the King of Kings,

Esus4 E
The Saviour of the world.

Chorus 2

A   Asus4 A   A/G   Asus4/G
‖: We seek Your face and _____ humble our - selves here.

A/G F#m7   Esus4 Bm
The fire of God consuming the hearts of man.

A   Asus4 A   A/G   Asus4/G
Nations will bow to You. _____ Kingdoms will shake before You.

A/G   F#m7 Esus4   Bm
We pray for re - vival,   we pray for re - vival. :‖

Interlude

‖: Bm | | F#m7 | | Esus4 | E :‖ *Play 5 times*
| E | | |

Chorus 3   *Repeat Chorus 2*

Outro

| A Asus2 | Asus4 A | A/G | Asus4/G A/G | |
| F#m7 | Esus4 | Bm | | ‖

The Reason I Live

Words and Music by
Marty Sampson

Je-sus, You are the rea-son I live. _

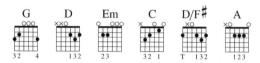

Chorus 1

N.C.
Jesus, You are the reason I live, whoa.

Jesus, You are the reason I live, yeah.

Jesus, You are the reason I live, whoa.

Jesus, You are the reason I live.

Verse 1

        G   **D**   **Em**
When I   think of the things ____ You've done for me,

       C   **G**   **D**
I know You are the reason I live.

       G   **D**   **Em**
And I,   I want to know ____ You more each day.

           C   **G**   **C**   **D**
God, please open my eyes, and show me Your way.

Pre-Chorus 1

Em   **C**
You are the reason I live in this world.

G   **D/F#**
You are the One that I want to be like.

Em   **C**
You are the reason I live in this world.

A   **C**   **A**   **C**
Show me the way to live,   I want to be like You.

Chorus 2

G   C   D   C
Jesus, You are the reason I live, whoa.

G   C   D   C
Jesus, You are the reason I live, yeah.

G   C   D   C
Jesus, You are the reason I live, whoa.

G   C   D   C
Jesus, You are the reason I live.

Verse 2   *Repeat Verse 1*

Pre-Chorus 2   *Repeat Pre-Chorus 1*

Chorus 3   *Repeat Chorus 2*

Bridge

Em   C   G
I'll always go Your way, and that will never change.

D/F♯   Em
You will be the One for all my days.

C   A
I'll always go Your way, and that will never change.

C   A   C
You will be the One for all of my days.

Chorus 4

G   C   D   C
‖: Jesus, You are the reason I live, whoa.

G   C   D   C
Jesus, You are the reason I live, yeah. :‖ *Play 7 times*

G   C   D   C
Jesus, You are the reason I live, whoa.

G   C   D   C
Jesus, You are the reason I live.

Rest In You

Words and Music by
Mia Fieldes

Melody:

Your faith-ful - ness ___

(Capo 2nd fret)

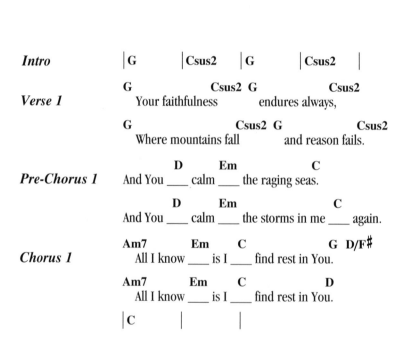

G   Csus2   D   Em   C   Am7   D/F#

Intro |G |Csus2 |G |Csus2 |

Verse 1
```
       G              Csus2 G          Csus2
       Your faithfulness      endures always,

       G                    Csus2 G          Csus2
       Where mountains fall        and reason fails.
```

Pre-Chorus 1
```
                   D      Em            C
       And You ___ calm ___ the raging seas.

                   D      Em                C
       And You ___ calm ___ the storms in me ___ again.
```

Chorus 1
```
       Am7        Em    C            G  D/F#
       All I know ___ is I ___ find rest in You.

       Am7        Em    C            D
       All I know ___ is I ___ find rest in You.
```

|C | | |

Verse 2

G   Csus2 G   Csus2
My heart will praise   throughout the night,

G   Csus2 G   Csus2
Where singing seems   a sacrifice.

Pre-Chorus 2   *Repeat Pre-Chorus 1*

Chorus 2

Am7   Em   C   G D/F♯
All I know ___ is I ___ find rest in You.

Am7   Em   C   D
All I know ___ is I ___ find rest in You.

Interlude   ‖: C | | G | :‖

Bridge

       C   D/F♯   Em
‖:   Your grace is all ___ I need.

C   D   Em
  Your grace is all ___ I need.   :‖

Chorus 3

   Am7   Em   C   G D/F♯
‖: All I know ___ is I ___ find rest in You.

Am7   Em   C   D
All I know ___ is I ___ find rest in You. :‖

Outro   ‖: C | | G | :‖ *Play 7 times*
         | C | | G   ‖

Saving Grace

Words and Music by
Michelle Fragar

Melody:

Night and day __ I seek Your __ face. __

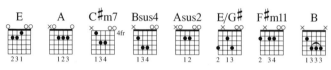

E   A   C#m7   Bsus4   Asus2   E/G#   F#m11   B

Intro | E | A | E | A |

Verse 1
      E   A
     Night and day I seek Your face,

      E   A
     Long for You in the secret place.

      E   A   C#m7   Bsus4   Asus2
     All I want in this life is to truly know ____ You more.

     | E | A |

Verse 2
      E   A
     As the waters cover the sea,

      E   A
     So Your love covers me,

      E   A
     Guiding me on roads unknown.

      C#m7   Bsus4   Asus2
     I trust in You ____ alone.

      C#m7   Bsus4   Asus2
     I trust in You ____ alone.

Chorus 1
                E/G# Asus2 Bsus4   E/G# Asus2 Bsus4
     My saving grace,   my endless love,

      C#m7   Bsus4   Asus2   F#m11   Bsus4
     Deeper and deep - er, I'm falling in love ____ with You.

                E/G# Asus2 Bsus4   E/G# Asus2 Bsus4
     My one desire,   my only truth,

      C#m7   Bsus4   Asus2   F#m11   Bsus4 B
     Deeper and deep - er, I'm falling in love ____ with You.

Verse 3	*Repeat Verse 2*

Chorus 2

   B **E/G♯ Asus2 Bsus4**   **E/G♯ Asus2 Bsus4**
My saving grace,   my endless love,

C♯m7   **Bsus4** **Asus2** **F♯m11** **Bsus4**
Deeper and deep - er, I'm falling in love ___ with You.

     E/G♯ Asus2 Bsus4 **E/G♯ Asus2 Bsus4**
My one desire,   my only truth,

C♯m7   **Bsus4** **Asus2** **F♯m11** **Bsus4 B**
Deeper and deep - er, I'm falling in love ___ with You.

Interlude

   E A Bsus4   **E** **A Bsus4**
With You. Falling in love ___ with You.

‖: **E** **A** | **Bsus4** :‖

Bridge

Asus2   **Bsus4 C♯m7 Asus2**
 And I will rise ___ on wings of ea - gles,

    Bsus4 **C♯m7** **Asus2**
Soaring high ___ above all my fears.

    Bsus4 **C♯m7** **Bsus4 B**
I rest in Your o - pen arms ___ of love.

Chorus 3	*Repeat Chorus 2*
Chorus 4	*Repeat Chorus 2*

Outro

E   **A**
 As the waters cover the sea,

E   **A**
 So Your love covers me.

‖: **Asus2** | **Bsus4** :‖ *Play 8 times*

Saviour King

Words and Music by
Marty Sampson and Mia Fieldes

Melody:

Let now the weak say I have

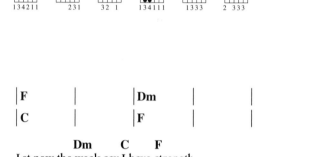

F   Dm   C   Gm   Bb   Gm7

Intro | F | | Dm | |
            | C | | F | |

Verse 1

                Dm   C   F
Let now the weak say I have strength

            Gm   Dm   C   F
By the Spirit of power that raised Christ from the dead.

               Dm   C   F
And now the poor stand and con - fess

            Gm   Dm   C   F
That my portion is Him and I'm more than blessed.

Pre-Chorus 1

Dm   Bb
   Let now our hearts burn with a flame,

                    F   C
A fire consuming all for Your Son's Holy Name,

Dm   Bb   Gm7 C
   And with the heavens we declare ____ You are our King.

Chorus 1

              F   Dm
We love You, ____ Lord. We worship You.

          C   F
You are our God, You alone are good.

Verse 2

        Dm   C   F
Let now Your church shine as the bride

      Gm   Dm   C   F
That You saw in Your heart as You offered up Your life.

       Dm   C   F   Gm   Dm
And now the lost be welcomed home by the saved and re - deemed,

      C   F
Those adopted as Your own.

Pre-Chorus 2   *Repeat Pre-Chorus 1*

Chorus 2   *Repeat Chorus 1*

Chorus 3

      F   Dm
You asked Your Son to carry this,

      C   F
The heavy cross, ____ our weight of ____ sin.

Chorus 4

      F   Dm
I love You, Lord, I worship You.

      C   F
Hope which was lost ____ now stands re - newed.

Chorus 5

      F   Dm
I give my life to honor this,

      C   F
The love of Christ, the Saviour ____ King.

Chorus 6   *Repeat Chorus 4*

Chorus 7   *Repeat Chorus 5*

Seeking You

Words and Music by
Marty Sampson

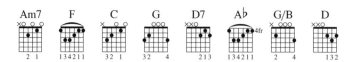

Am7   F   C   G   D7   A♭   G/B   D

Intro |Am7 F C| |Am7 F C| |

               Am7 F   C

Verse 1   It's You I can't es - cape.

                              Am7   F   C

               Your love has me sur - rounded in ev'ry way.

                      Am7   F   C

               So I surrender now and raise ___ my hands.

                    Am7 F C

               All I want is You.

               Am7   F   C

Verse 2   You have carried me

                             Am7   F   C

               Through many storms and many rag - ing seas.

                    Am7   F   C

               You rescue me in my hour ___ of need,

                    Am7 G F

               All I want is You.

Chorus 1

C
I'm coming to You for the love that I need,

D7
I'm desperate for Your touch.

                F A♭   C G/B Am7 A♭
I'm seeking You,   I'm seeking You.

|C   G/B |Am7 A♭ ‖:Am7 F C | :‖

Verse 3

Am7   F   C
You are always by my side,

                  Am7   F   C
My closest friend, in You I can ____ re - ly.

                    Am7   F   C
You're with me ev'ry moment of ___ my life.

           Am7 G F
All I want is You.

Chorus 2

           C
‖: I'm coming to You for the love that I need,

D7
I'm desperate for Your touch.

                F A♭   C G/B Am7 A♭
I'm seeking You,   I'm seeking You.   :‖

Interlude

‖:C G/B |Am7 A♭ :‖ *Play 3 times*

Bridge

D   F
  And all I want is   more of You.

D   F
  And all I want is to be with You.

Chorus 3

Repeat Chorus 2

Outro

‖:C G/B |Am7 A♭ :‖ *Play 7 times*
|C   ‖

Shout Unto God

Words and Music by
Joel Houston and Marty Sampson

'Cause the en-e-my has been de-feat - ed

(Capo 2nd fret)

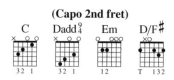

Intro |C |Dadd$^9_4$ |C |Dadd$^9_4$ |

Verse 1
                C
‖: 'Cause the enemy has been defeated

      Dadd$^9_4$
And death couldn't hold You down,

          C
We're gonna lift our voice in victory,

         Dadd$^9_4$
We're gonna make Your praises loud. :‖ *Play 4 times*

Verse 2
                C
‖: 'Cause the enemy has been defeated
      (Shout unto God with a voice of triumph.)

      Dadd$^9_4$
And death couldn't hold You down.
      (Shout unto God with a voice of praise.)

          C
We're gonna lift our voice in victory,
      (Shout unto God with a voice of triumph.)

         Dadd$^9_4$
We're gonna make Your praises loud.
      (We lift Your name up, we lift Your name up.) :‖

Chorus 1

C
Shout unto God with a voice of triumph.

Shout unto God with a voice of praise.

Shout unto God with a voice of triumph.

We lift Your name up, we lift Your name up.

Chorus 2

C
‖:   Shout unto God with a voice of triumph.

Dadd$^9_4$
Shout unto God with a voice of praise.

Em
Shout unto God with a voice of triumph.

D/F♯
We lift your name up, we lift Your name up. :‖ *Play 4 times*

| C   ‖

Sing (Your Love)

Words and Music by
Reuben Morgan

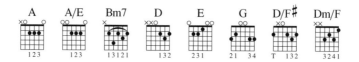

Intro

‖: A |A/E |Bm7 |D   :‖

Verse 1

A   E   Bm7   D
It used to be dark - ness   without You.

A   E   Bm7   D
I lived my life in blind - ness,   but now I'm found.

Chorus 1

          A   A/E   E   Bm7
And I'll sing, sing ____ I love You so.

D   A
And I'll sing,

               G   D/F♯   Dm/F
Because the world ____ can't take away ____ Your love.

Intro

|A |A/E |Bm7 |D |

Verse 2

A   E   Bm7   D
Found me in weak - ness,   broken.

A   E   Bm7   D
You came to me in kind - ness,   and now I live.

Chorus 2	**A A/E E Bm7**
	‖: And I'll sing, sing ___ I love You so.
	
	D **A**
	  And I'll sing,
	
	          G **D/F♯** **Dm/F**
	Because the world ___ can't take away ___ Your love. :‖

Interlude 1	‖: **A** |**E** |**Bm7** |**D** :‖

Bridge	**A** **E** **Bm7**
	‖: I'll give my life for You, ___ Lord,
	
	D
	  For all You've done. :‖ ***Play 3 times***
	
	    A **E** **Bm7** **D**
	I'll give my life for You, ___ Lord.

Chorus 3	*Repeat Chorus 2*
Interlude 2	*Repeat Interlude 1*
Outro	**A** **E** **Bm7** ‖: I'll give my life for You, ___ Lord, **D** For all You've done. :‖ ***Play 4 times*** |**A** ‖

Sovereign Hands

Words and Music by
Mia Fieldes

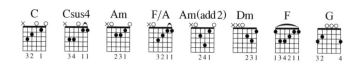

Intro

| C Csus4 | C Csus4 | C Csus4 | C Csus4 |

Verse 1

C Csus4   C Csus4
Sov'reign hands

Am F/A   Am(add2)
Nailed to a hum - ble cross.

C Csus4   C Csus4
Scars You bear

Am F/A   Am(add2)
Speak of Your redeem - ing love.

Pre-Chorus 1

Dm   F   C   G
No won - der I call ____ You Sav - iour.

Dm   F
No wonder I'm sing - ing.

Chorus 1

G   Dm
God of all the heav - ens,

                F   C
Now and 'til forev - er, high above the u - niverse.

G   Dm
God of our redemp - tion,

                F   C
God of my surren - der, the glory is ____ Yours.

Verse 2

```
C  Csus4        C  Csus4
    Sov'reign God,

Am  F/A              A(add2)
    Laying down a ho - ly life.

C  Csus4        C  Csus4
    Heaven's Son,

Am  F/A          Am(add2)
    Willing to be crucified.
```

Pre-Chorus 2   *Repeat Pre-Chorus 1*

Chorus 2   *Repeat Chorus 1*

Bridge

```
G     Dm     F        C
  Holy,   holy,   holy Lord.

G     Dm     F        C
  Holy,   holy,   holy Lord.
| C  Csus4 | C  Csus4 |
```

Verse 3

```
C  Csus4        C  Csus4
    Open hands

C  Csus4        C      Csus4
    Given to a sov - 'reign cause.

C  Csus4   C  Csus4
    All I am,

C  Csus4            Am(add2)
    God, will be for - ever Yours.
```

Pre-Chorus 3   *Repeat Pre-Chorus 1*

Chorus 3   *Repeat Chorus 1*

Chorus 4   *Repeat Chorus 1*

Outro

```
G     Dm     F        C
  Holy,   holy,   holy Lord.

G     Dm     F        C
  Holy,   holy,   holy Lord.
```

The Stand

Words and Music by
Joel Houston

Melody:

You stood be - fore ___ cre - a - tion,

(Capo 2nd fret)

G   C   G/B   Em   Cmaj7   Am7   D

Intro
| G | | | | | | | | | | |

Verse 1
 G   C
You stood before creation, e - ternity in Your hand.

  G/B   Em   C
And You spoke the earth into mo - tion, my soul now ___ to stand.

Verse 2
  Cmaj7 G
    You stood before my failure

  C
And carried the cross for my shame.

  G/B   Em   C
My sin weighed upon Your shoul - ders, my soul now ___ to stand.

Pre-Chorus 1
  Cmaj7   C Am7   Em
  So what could I say, and what could I do

          C   D   Em
But offer this heart, ___ O God, completely ___ to You?

Verse 3
  G   C
So I'll walk upon salvation, Your Spirit alive in me.

  G/B   Em   C
This life to declare Your prom - ise, my soul now ___ to stand.

Pre-Chorus 2 *Repeat Pre-Chorus 1*

Pre-Chorus 3

                     C Am7   Em
So what could I say,   and what could I do

G   Am7   D   C   G D Em
But offer this heart, ___ O God,   completely ___ to You?

Interlude   ‖: C   G | D   Em   :‖ *Play 7 times*

Chorus

              C   G   D   Em
‖:   So I'll stand with arms high and heart abandoned

C   G   D   Em
In awe of the One who gave it all.

C   G   D   Em
I'll stand, my soul, Lord, to You surrendered.

C   G   D Em
All I am ___ is Yours.   :‖ *Play 4 times*

C   G   D   Em
So I'll stand with arms high and heart abandoned

C   G   D   Em
In awe of the One who gave it all.

C   G   D   Em
I'll stand, my soul, Lord, to You surrendered.

C   G   D
All I am ___ is Yours.

Outro

                     C Am7   Em
So what could I say,   and what could I do

G   Am7   D   Em
But offer this heart, ___ O God,   completely to You?

Take All Of Me

Words and Music by
Marty Sampson

Melody:

And I love You, _

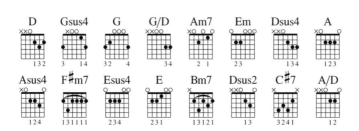

D   Gsus4   G   G/D   Am7   Em   Dsus4   A

Asus4   F#m7   Esus4   E   Bm7   Dsus2   C#7   A/D

Intro |D |

                   Gsus4 G   G/D D

Chorus 1   ‖: And I love   You, all of my hope is in   You.

                 Am7   Em   Dsus4 D

          Jesus Christ, ___ take my life, ___ take all of me.   :‖

          ‖: A Asus4 |A Asus4 :‖

                   A   Asus4

Verse 1   You broke the night like the sun

                   A   Asus4   F#m7

          And healed my heart with Your ___ great love.

          D   A   Asus4

           And any trouble I couldn't bear,

                 A   Asus4   Esus4 E

          You lifted me upon Your shoulders.

                 Bm7   A   E

Pre-Chorus 1 Love that's strong - er, love that cov - ers sin

                D   Bm7

          And takes ___ the weight of the world.

Chorus 2

    Asus4 A   Esus4   E
I love   You, all of my hope is in ___ You.

            Bm7   F#m7   Esus4 E
Jesus Christ, ___ take my life, ___ take all of me.

| Dsus2 | | |

Verse 2

            A   D
Stand on mountaintops with me,

A   D   F#m7 D F#m7 D
  With You I walk through the val - leys.

             A   D
You gave Your only Son for me,

A   D   Esus4   E
  Your grace is all I rely ___ on.

Pre-Chorus 2   *Repeat Pre-Chorus 1*

Chorus 3

    Asus4 A   Esus4   E Esus4
‖: I love   You, all of my hope is in ___ You.

E   Bm7   F#m7   Esus4 E
Jesus Christ, ___ take my life, ___ take all of me.   :‖

Interlude

| Asus4 A | Asus4 A | E | |
| Bm7 | F#m7 | Esus4 | E |

Bridge

    Asus4 A   E   F#m7   D
I love   You so, ___ and I give ___ up my heart ___ to say

            A   C#7
I need ___ You so,

       F#m7 E   D   A E A/D Bm7
My ev - 'ry - thing, ___ O God.

Outro

‖: A | E | A/D | Bm7   :‖
| A   ‖

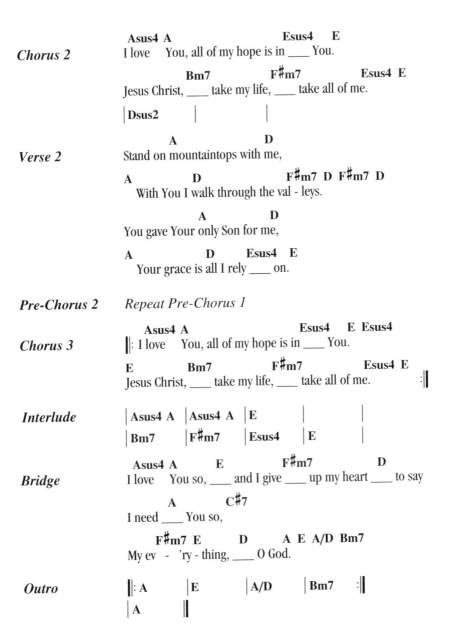

Take It All

Words and Music by Matt Crocker,
Marty Sampson and Scott Ligertwood

Melody:

Search-ing the world, __ the lost will be found. __

B G#m E F# C#m

1 3 3 3   1 3 4 1 1 1   2 3 1   1 3 4 2 1 1   1 3 4 2 1

Intro ‖: N.C.(B) | | | :‖

Verse 1
N.C.(B)
Searching the world, the lost will be found.

In freedom we live, as one we cry out.

You carried the cross, You died and rose again.

My God, I'll only ever give my all.

Verse 2
N.C.(B)
You sent Your Son, from heaven to earth.

You delivered us all, it's eternally heard.

                                                              G#m
I searched for truth, and all I found was You.

                         E
My God, I'll only ever give my all.

Chorus 1
B   F#
   Jesus, we're livin' for Your name.
   G#m   E
We'll never be ashamed of You.
B   F#
   Our praise and all we are today,
C#m N.C.
Take, take, take it all.

Take, take, take it all.

‖: N.C.(B) | :‖

Verse 3   *Repeat Verse 2*

Chorus 2

     B   **F#**
‖: Jesus, we're livin' for Your name.

    G#m   **E**
We'll never be ashamed of You.

B   **F#**
  Our praise and all we are today,

C#m N.C.
Take, take, take it all.

                      B
Take, take, take it all. :‖

Bridge

    C#m   **G#m F#**   **E**
‖: Running to the One   who heals the blind,

C#m   **G#m**   **F#**
Following the shin - ing light

C#m   **G#m F#**   **E**   **B**
In Your hands the power to save the world and my life. :‖

Chorus 3

     B   **F#**
‖: Jesus, we're livin' for Your name.

    G#m   **E**
We'll never be ashamed of You.

B   **F#**
  Our praise and all we are today,

C#m N.C.
Take, take, take it all.

Take, take, take it all. :‖ *Play 3 times*

                      B
Take, take, take it all.

Tell The World

Words and Music by Marty Sampson,
Joel Houston and Jonathon Douglass

Melody:

Don't wan - na stand here and shout Your praise

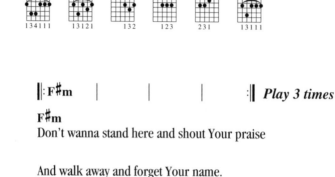

F#m   Bm7   D   A   E   B9(no3rd)

Intro

‖: F#m | | | :‖ *Play 3 times*

Verse 1

F#m
Don't wanna stand here and shout Your praise

And walk away and forget Your name.

I stand for You if it's all I do,

'Cause there is none that compares to You.

Pre-Chorus 1

F#m
'Cause all I want in this lifetime is You.

               Bm7 D
And all I want in this whole world is You, You, You.

Chorus 1

A   E
Tell the world that Jesus lives.

F#m   D
Tell the world that, tell the world that.

A   E
Tell the world that He died for them.

F#m   D
Tell the world that He lives again.

| F#m | | | | |

Verse 2

F#m
No longer I, but Christ in me,

'Cause it's the truth that set me free.

How could this world be a better place

By Thy mercy, by Thy grace.

Pre-Chorus 2   *Repeat Pre-Chorus 1*

Chorus 2

   A   E
‖: Tell the world that Jesus lives.
F#m   D
  Tell the world that,   tell the world that.
A   E
  Tell the world that He died for them.
F#m   D
  Tell the world that He lives again. :‖

Bridge

N.C.
Come on, come on, we'll tell the world about You.

Come on, come on, we'll tell the world about You.

         A   B9(no3rd)   F#m D
‖: Come on, ___ come on, we'll tell ___ the world about You.
         A   B9(no3rd)   F#m D
Come on, ___ come on, we'll tell ___ the world about You.   :‖

Chorus 3   *Repeat Chorus 2*

Outro

         A   E   F#m
‖: Come on, ___ come on, we'll tell ___ the world about You.
            D
Tell the world that,   tell the world that. :‖
         A   Bm7   F#m
Come on, ___ come on, we'll tell ___ the world about You.
            D
Tell the world that,   tell the world that.
         A   E   F#m
Come on, ___ come on, we'll tell ___ the world about You.
            D   N.C.
Tell the world that,   tell the world that. About You.

The Time Has Come

Words and Music by
Joel Houston

Melody:

I found love   be - yond all   rea - son.

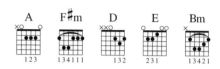

A   F♯m   D   E   Bm

| | |
123 134111 132 231 13421

Intro | A | | | |

Verse 1
    A
I found love beyond all reason.

                           F♯m
You gave Your life, You're all for me.

    D   **A**
And called me Yours forev - er,

Caught in the mercy fallout.

                         F♯m
I found hope, found life, found all I need,

D   **A**
'Cause You're all I need.

Pre-Chorus 1
    E   **F♯m**   **D**
The time has come to stand for all we believe ___ in.

    E   **F♯m**   **D**
So I, for one, am gonna give my praise to You, ___ Jesus.

GUITAR CHORD SONGBOOK

Chorus 1

                 A
Today, ____ today it's all or nothing.

F#m   **D**
All the way, the praise goes out to You.

                              A
Yeah, all the praise goes out to You.

Today, today I live for one thing,

   F#m   **D**
To give You praise in ev'rything I do.

                              A
Yeah, all the praise goes out to You.

Verse 2   *Repeat Verse 1*

Pre-Chorus 2   *Repeat Pre-Chorus 1*

Chorus 2   *Repeat Chorus 1*

Interlude

‖: F#m |D |A | :‖
‖: F#m | |Bm | :‖

Bridge

   F#m
‖:   All we are is Yours.

Bm   **D**
   All we're living for is all ____ You are,

       A   **E**
Is all ____ that You are. :‖ *Play 3 times*

Pre-Chorus 3

           E   **F#m**   **D**
‖: The time ____ has come to stand for all we believe ____ in.

   E   **F#m**   **D**
So I, for one, am gonna give my praise to You. :‖ Jesus.

Chorus 3   *Repeat Chorus 1*

Outro

              F#m   **D**   **A**
Ev'rything I do, ____ yeah, all the praise goes out to You.

              F#m   **D**   **A**
Ev'rything I do, ____ yeah, all the praise goes out to You.

To The Ends Of The Earth

Words and Music by
Marty Sampson and Joel Houston

Em7   Cadd9   G   D   Am7   Fadd9

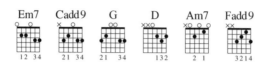

Intro

‖: **Em7 Cadd9** |**G   D** |**Em7 Cadd9** |**G   D** :‖

Verse 1

Em7   Cadd9 G   D   Em7 Cadd9
Love unfail - ing, ___ overtak - ing my heart.

G   D
You take me in.

Em7   Cadd9   G   D   Cadd9
Finding peace ___ again,   fear is lost ___ in all You ___ are.

Pre-Chorus 1

D   Em7
And I would give the world to tell Your sto - ry,

Cadd9
'Cause I know that You've called ___ me,

G
I know that You've called ___ me.

D   Cadd9
I've lost myself for good within Your prom - ise,

Em7   Cadd9
And I won't hide ___ it. I won't hide it.

Chorus 1

G
Jesus, I believe in You,

      D   **Am7**
And I would go to the ends of the earth,

      Cadd9
To the ends of the earth.

         G
For You ____ alone are the Son of God,

      Fadd9
And all the world will see

         Am7   **Cadd9**
That You are ____ God, that You are ____ God.

Interlude 1 |Em7 Cadd9 |G   D |Em7 Cadd9 |G   D |

Verse 2   *Repeat Verse 1*

Pre-Chorus 2   *Repeat Pre-Chorus 1*

Chorus 2   *Repeat Chorus 1*

Interlude 2   ‖: Em7 Cadd9 |G   D :‖ *Play 6 times*

Chorus 3

      G
‖: Jesus, I believe in You,

      D   **Am7**
And I would go to the ends of the earth,

      Cadd9
To the ends of the earth.

         G
For You ____ alone are the Son of God,

      Fadd9   **Am7**
And all the world will see that You are ____ God,

        Cadd9
That You are ____ God. :‖ *Play 3 times*

What The World Will Never Take

Words and Music by Matt Crocker,
Marty Sampson and Scott Ligertwood

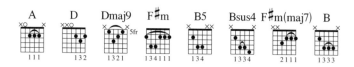

Intro

‖: A | | D | :‖

Verse 1

A
With all I'm holding inside,

D
With all my hopes and desires,

A
And all the dreams that I've dreamt.

With all I am hoping to be,

D
And all that the world would bring,

Dmaj9
And all that fails to compare,

F#m   **B5**   **Dmaj9**
You say You want all of me.

A   **B5**   **A**
I wouldn't have it any other way.

Chorus 1

A
I've got a Saviour and He's living in me.

D   F#m Bsus4   D   A
Whoa, ___ I wanna know,   I wanna know You to - day.

And You're the best thing that has happened to me

F#m   Bsus4   D   A
And the world will never take, the world will never take You a - way.

| A | | D | | |

Verse 2

A
With all I'm hoping to be,

              D
With all that the world would bring

           Dmaj9
And all that fails to compare,

F#m   B5   Dmaj9
You say You want all of me.

      A   B5   A
I wouldn't have it any other way.

Chorus 2

  A
||: I've got a Saviour and He's living in me.

D   F#m Bsus4   D   A
Whoa, ___ I wanna know,   I wanna know You to - day.

And You're the best thing that has happened to me

F#m   Bsus4   D   A
And the world will never take, the world will never take You a - way. :||

Interlude

||: F#m | F#m(maj7) | A | B | :||
| | | |

Chorus 3

Repeat Chorus 2

Outro

A   D   A
No one could ever take You a - way.

          D   A
No one could ever take You a - way.

Where The Love Lasts Forever

Words and Music by
Joel Houston

Melody:

Your mer - cy found _ me

Chord diagrams: D, G, Bm, Asus4, A, D/F#

Intro

‖: D | G | Bm | Asus4 A :‖

Verse 1

D   G   Bm
 Your mercy found me upon the broken road

          A
And lifted me beyond ____ my failing.

D   G   Bm
 Into Your glory my sin and shame dissolved

          A
And now forever Yours ____ I'll stand.

Pre-Chorus 1

    D/F# G   A
In love nev - er to end,

  Bm   D/F#
To call You more than Lord,

  G   Asus4 A
Glo - rious Friend.

Chorus 1

      D   G   Bm   A
So I'll throw ____ my life ____ upon all ____ that You are,

       D   G   Bm A
'Cause I know ____ You gave ____ it all for me.

      D/F#   G
And when all ____ else fades,

     A   Bm   D/F#
My soul ____ will dance ____ with You

      G   Asus4 A
Where the love lasts forev - er.

| D | G | Bm | Asus4 A | |

Verse 2	*Repeat Verse 1*
Pre-Chorus 2	*Repeat Pre-Chorus 1*

Chorus 2

```
          D              G            Bm            A
‖: So I'll throw ___ my life ___ upon all ___ that You are,

          D              G            Bm  A
'Cause I know ___ You gave ___ it all for me.

          D/F♯           G
And when all ___ else fades,

          A            Bm          D/F♯
My soul ___ will dance ___ with You

          G              Asus4  A
Where the love lasts forev - er.        :‖
```

Interlude

```
| Bm      | G        | D/F♯     | A         |
| Bm      | G        | D/F♯     | Asus4     |
```

Bridge

```
          Bm             G
And forev - er I will sing,

          D/F♯           A
Lord, forev - er I will sing,

               Bm              G
How You gave ___ Your life away

          D/F♯                 Asus4    A
Just to save ___ me, Lord, You saved ___ me.
```

Chorus 3	*Repeat Chorus 2*

Outro

```
D/F♯       G            Asus4  A              D/F♯
  Where the love lasts forev - er,    I will be with You.

          G            Asus4  A              D/F♯
Where the love lasts forev - er,    I will sing to You.

          G            Asus4  A              D/F♯
Where the love lasts forev - er,    I will dance with You.

          G            A
Where the love lasts forev - er.
```

There Is Nothing Like

Words and Music by
Jonas Myrin and Marty Sampson

Melody:

Fa-ther true _ and mer - ci - ful, _

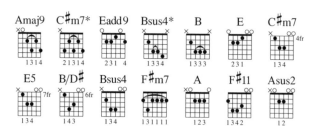

Amaj9 C#m7* Eadd9 Bsus4* B E C#m7
E5 B/D# Bsus4 F#m7 A F#11 Asus2

Intro

| Amaj9 | C#m7* Amaj9 | Eadd9 | Bsus4* B | |
| Amaj9 | C#m7* Amaj9 | E | B | |
‖: C#m7 E5 | B/D# Bsus4 | C#m7 E5 | B/D# Bsus4 :‖

Verse 1

C#m7   E5   B/D# Bsus4
Father true ____ and mer - ciful,

C#m7   E5   B/D# Bsus4
Bound to me ____ with love.

   C#m7   E5   B/D#   Bsus4 C#m7 E5 B/D# Bsus4
A - dopted in, ____ free ____ from all sin.

Verse 2

C#m7 E5   B/D#   Bsus4
Jesus, Sav - iour, glo - rified,

   C#m7   E5   B/D# Bsus4
Your offering, none ____ could give.

  C#m7   E5   B/D#   Bsus4 C#m7 E5 B/D# Bsus4
I stand before ____ You hum - bled and in awe.

Pre-Chorus 1

F#m7   A
And all ____ to You, God,

C#m7   E   F#11
For all ____ You are to me.

Chorus 1

              A   C#m7 A
There is nothing like, there is nothing like

          E   B
Your love, ____ Your love.

              A   C#m7 A
There is nothing like, there is nothing like

          E   F#11
Your love, ____ Your love.

Interlude 1

‖: C#m7 E5 | B/D# Bsus4 :‖

Verse 3

C#m7   E5   B/D#   Bsus4
Holy Spir - it, gift ____ of God,

C#m7   E5   B/D# Bsus4
Teach my soul ____ to soar.

C#m7   E5   B/D#   Bsus4 C#m7 E5 B/D# Bsus4
Train me in ____ Your ho - ly ways, O Lord.

Pre-Chorus 2   *Repeat Pre-Chorus 1*

Chorus 2   *Repeat Chorus 1*

Chorus 3   *Repeat Chorus 1*

Interlude 2   ‖: Asus2 | C#m7 Bsus4 | Asus2 | C#m7 Bsus4 :‖

Bridge

        Asus2   C#m7   Bsus4
‖: I'll love You forever, I'll love You for - ever.

        Asus2   C#m7 Bsus4
I'll love You forever, Lord.   :‖

        N.C.
‖: I'll love You forever, I'll love You forever. :‖

        Asus2   C#m7   Bsus4
I'll love You forever, I'll love You for - ever.

        Asus2   C#m7   B/D#
I'll love You forever, I'll love You for - ever.

Interlude 3   ‖: F#m7 C#m7 │ B   │ F#m7 C#m7 │ B/D#   :‖

Pre-Chorus 3

        F#m7   A
‖: And all ___ to You, God,

        C#m7   E   F#11
For all ___ You are to me.   :‖

Chorus 3

                  A   C#m7 A
‖: There is nothing like, there is nothing like

           E   B
Your love, ___ Your love.

                A   C#m7 A
There is nothing like, there is nothing like

           E   F#11
Your love, ___ Your love.   :‖

           A
Your love.